Monitoring poverty and social exclusion 2005

I Guy Palmer, Jane Carr and Peter Kenway

JOSEPH ROWNTREE
FOUNDATION

np
new Policy Institute

poverty.org.uk

Much of the data used in this report was made available through the UK Data Archive. Neither the original collectors of the data nor the Archive bear any responsibility for the analyses presented here.

The same applies for all datasets used in this report, including those from the Department of Health, the Department for Education and Skills, the Department for Work and Pensions, the Office of the Deputy Prime Minister, the Home Office, the General Register Office for Scotland, the Welsh Assembly, the Scottish Executive, and the Office for National Statistics.

The **Joseph Rowntree Foundation** has supported this project as part of its programme of research and innovative development projects, which it hopes will be of value to policy makers, practitioners and service users. The facts presented and views expressed in this report are, however, those of the authors and not necessarily those of the Foundation.

Joseph Rowntree Foundation
The Homestead
40 Water End
York YO30 6WP
Website: www.jrf.org.uk

ISBN   1 85935 395 9 (paperback, English language edition)
        1 85935 396 7 (pdf, English language edition: available at www.jrf.org.uk)
        1 85935 406 8 (paperback, Welsh language edition)
        1 85935 407 6 (pdf, Welsh language edition: available at www.jrf.org.uk)

A CIP catalogue record for this report is available from the British Library.

Designed by Adkins Design

Further copies of this report, or any other JRF publication, can be obtained either from the JRF website (www.jrf.org.uk/bookshop/) or from our distributor, York Publishing Services, 64 Hallfield Road, York YO31 7ZQ (Tel: 01904 430033).

Monitoring poverty
and social exclusion 2005

· · · · · · · · · · · · · · · · · · ·

Contents

Introduction

The Monitoring Poverty and Social Exclusion series

This is the seventh in a series of regular reports which began in 1998. Its aim is to provide an independent assessment of the progress being made in eliminating poverty and reducing social exclusion in Britain. This report follows the previous ones in all essential respects, namely:

- 50 indicators each containing two graphs, the first of which typically shows progress over time while the second shows how the problem varies between different groups within the population, divided variously according to either income level, social class, economic or family status, gender, ethnicity, and so on.
- The indicators are grouped in a series of themes and the themes into six chapters. Four of the chapters are focused on particular age groups within the population, namely children, young adults aged under 25, adults aged 25 to retirement and adults above retirement. In addition, there is an opening chapter on the subject of income and a closing one on the subject of community.

There are also two sets of four maps, the first covering Great Britain and the second covering England only.

These reports are only one part of the output of *Monitoring Poverty and Social Exclusion*. Besides these reports, there have been two separate reports for Scotland, in 2002 and 2004, and a separate report for Wales, published in November 2005.

www.poverty.org.uk

In their turn, all of these reports are themselves only a small subset of the complete set of indicators which have been created as part of this project, all of which are available on the project website www.poverty.org.uk. At the last count, the website contained more than 600 graphs and around 50 maps, drawing on a combined databank some 40Gb in size. *Monitoring Poverty and Social Exclusion* has therefore become a substantial and, we hope, high quality resource whose principal weakness is that not enough is made of it.

Anybody interested in any of the material in this report should, if they wish to explore further, visit the website. Anybody wishing to reproduce material from the report is also encouraged to visit the website to check that there is not a more up-to-date version of the graph. While the reports come out no more than annually, the graphs on the website are updated within a few weeks of the data being published. The data behind every graph is also available on the website.

The focus of this report

The fact that there are many hundreds of graphs behind this report means that what is presented here is but a small selection of what is available. What has guided that selection?

Most of the subjects selected for this report are similar to those in the last report in 2003. There are some new graphs: the importance of cars is one; the acquisition of further qualifications year by year after age 16 is a second; levels of benefit take-up is a third. There is also more material on various aspects of work, reflecting the way in which 'in-work' poverty is becoming ever more important. In spite of these changes, however, the overall list of indicators this time is little different from last time.

Where the major difference lies is in how each subject has been broken down to show how the incidence differs between different groups. One of the major themes of the last report was the variations between the English regions, Wales and Scotland. This report, by contrast, has almost nothing to say on this subject (but see the website). Instead, the breakdowns here have been chosen to highlight how things vary according to:

- the household's economic status (whether working or not and if working, how much);
- whether the household includes dependent children or not;
- whether one or more of the working-age adults in the household is disabled or not;
- for various aspects of work, what the individual's highest level of qualification is.

In their turn, these choices reflect the two major chosen themes for this year's report, namely: child poverty and what can be done to bring it down further; and the particular situation of disabled people of working age and how far work can be the answer to their poverty.

The geographical scope of the report

Wherever data sources permit, the scope of this report is the United Kingdom; that is England, Wales, Scotland and Northern Ireland. In many cases, however, only analysis at a Great Britain level (ie not including Northern Ireland) is possible. Furthermore, in some cases even the data from England, Scotland and Wales is not comparable. One example is education, where the examination system in Scotland is different from that in both England and Wales. In other cases, one or both of the legislation and/or its interpretation may be different, and even if things have the same name comparing them, never mind adding them together, is unwise. In this context, some of the graphs are restricted to England and Wales, and sometimes to England only.

Commentary

There are many ways of presenting the 100 graphs and eight maps that make up the body of this report. The chapters themselves, organised around different age groups within the population – children, young adults aged under 25, adults aged 25 to retirement, and pensioners – is one way of doing it. This commentary, by contrast, does it differently, with its principal focus on just a few major themes. The two principal themes are child poverty and poverty among disabled people.

- Child poverty has been chosen because, with the definitive numbers showing whether the government met its first child poverty target due early in 2006, now is a good moment to start looking forward, to what extra needs to be done if the next child poverty target, set for 2010, is to be realised.
- Poverty and disability has been chosen because of the current review of the benefits arrangements for disabled people of working age. The situation of disabled people is one that has received little attention yet where there is a wealth of interesting and significant information.

Both of these themes are closely connected with work: much of the growing body of material contained in these reports on that subject is therefore subsumed within these two thematic discussions. Given the broad scope of these reports, however, there is still a lot of material that falls outside of these two discussions. As a result, the commentary opens with an overview discussion of poverty as it affects all the different groups within society and it closes with a discussion of other topics, namely educational qualifications, health inequalities, crime, housing and geographical patterns.

The last of these reflects upon the geographical patterns revealed in two panels of four maps, one for Britain as a whole and one for England, this special treatment of England reflecting the fact that there are separate reports in the series for Wales and Scotland.

Throughout this commentary, the indicators are referred to by the graph number and whether the graph is the first (A) or the second (B) graph of the pair. The maps are referred to either as GB1-4 or E1-4, for Great Britain and England respectively.

Poverty overview
Poverty incomes
The main measure of income poverty used in this report is a household income that is 60 per cent or less of the average (median) household income in that year. The latest year for which data is available is 2003/04. In that year the 60 per cent threshold was worth:

- £180 per week for a two adult household;
- £100 per week for a single adult;
- £260 per week for two adults living with two children;
- £180 per week for a single adult living with two children.

This sum of money is after income tax and national insurance have been deducted from earnings and after council tax, rent, mortgage and water charges have been paid. It is therefore what a household has available to spend on everything else it needs, from food and heating to travel and entertainment.

Defining the poverty threshold in relation to income in the current year produces what is commonly known as a 'relative' measure of poverty. While this is in some ways a misleading term – any measure of poverty is inherently relative – it is important to check progress against both relative and fixed thresholds. The fixed threshold used here is 60 per cent of average household income in 1996/97, uplifted when making comparisons in later years only for price inflation.

The number of people in income poverty

In 2003/04, 12 million people in Britain were living in income poverty, about one in every five. This number is nearly two million below its peak in the early 1990s and lower than at any time since 1987. It is, however, still nearly twice what it was at the end of the 1970s. [1A] Of this 12 million, 3¹/2 million are children, just over 2¹/2 million are adults who live with those children, 2 million are pensioners and just over 3¹/2 million are working-age adults living without any dependent children. [2B]

The strong and steady decline in the number of people living below a fixed low income threshold is a sign that even where people continue to live in income poverty, their income has nevertheless increased. [1A] Both the extent of poverty and the depth of poverty have therefore declined.

Poverty rates

The term 'poverty rate' is used here to mean the proportion of each group of people living in income poverty.

Since the mid-1990s, poverty rates have come down significantly for both pensioners (27 per cent down to 22 per cent) and families with children (child poverty down from 32 per cent to 29 per cent). By contrast, the poverty rate for working-age adults without dependent children (17 per cent) is, at best, unchanged. [2A] Since the number of people in this group is actually growing, the number of working-age adults without dependent children who are in poverty is actually up by 400,000 since the late 1990s. [3A]

The group for whom the poverty rate has fallen furthest are single pensioners (32 per cent down to 21 per cent). This is because the 'guaranteed' level of Pension Credit (Income Support in all but name) for single pensioners is now generally above the income poverty line. Single pensioners are now no more likely than pensioner couples to be living in poverty. [35A]

Concentrations of poverty

The report provides a number of indications on the extent to which income poverty is concentrated in particular places.

- 50 per cent of the people with low incomes live in just 20 per cent of small local areas, with the other 50 per cent living outside of these areas. [43A]
- Coincidentally, 50 per cent of children of primary school age who are entitled to free school meals (that is, children from a low income household usually without work) are concentrated in 20 per cent of schools. This figure for 2005 is the same as the one for 1996. [9A] Despite the fall in child poverty over that period, the degree to which children from poor homes are concentrated in a minority of schools remains unchanged.
- By contrast, the proportion of households in council or housing association accommodation who have a low income has come down since the mid-1990s, from 54 per cent in 1996/97 to 46 per cent in 2003/04. This level is, however, still far higher than among those in private accommodation (renting or owning) where the figure is now 16 per cent. [42A]
- Inner London has by the far the most extreme distribution of household incomes anywhere in the country. Thirty-three per cent of households in Inner London are in the poorest fifth of households nationally, a figure quite unmatched anywhere else in the country, while a further 30 per cent have incomes that are in the richest fifth nationally. [1B]

Child poverty

The 2004/05 child poverty target

In March 2006, when the next set of official poverty statistics are published, the question of whether the government has reached its principal short-term poverty target, to reduce child poverty by a quarter by 2004/05, will at last receive a definitive answer.

The latest figures, for 2003/04, show child poverty standing at 3.5 million. The government's target for 2004/05 represents 3.1 million children. When the target was set in 1999, child poverty stood at 4.1 million. This means that child poverty is down 600,000 from the start date, leaving a further 400,000 to go in the final year of the period. [7A]

With the definitive answer so close, there is no point in speculating whether the 2004/05 target will be reached. What matters now is what needs to be done to reach the government's next target, of reducing child poverty by a half (to bring it down to 2 million) by 2010. [7A] The following three features of the present situation are crucial to this. They are:

● the importance of higher employment overall in reducing poverty;
● the level of in-work poverty;
● the level of worklessness among lone parent families.

The importance of employment

First, it is the increase in employment since 1997 rather than the increase in benefits which is primarily responsible for the fall in the rates of child poverty.

Even though benefits for households with children are about 10 per cent higher, relative to earnings, than they were a decade ago [4A], the risk (rate) of poverty for a working-age household of a given work status is, if anything, actually slightly higher than it was then. [22A] So, for example, reliance on out-of-work benefits still leaves most households with children below the income poverty line.

What has brought poverty down among working-age households is the shift from groups with the highest risk of poverty – the unemployed and 'other workless' (chiefly lone parents and sick and disabled) – to lower risk ones, that is where someone in the household is doing some paid work. Unemployment as a cause of working-age poverty has come down particularly sharply. [22B]

In-work benefits too, in the shape of tax credits, have played only a limited direct role in lifting households out of poverty. Just 20 per cent of households getting Working Tax Credit or Child Tax Credit (above the flat £10 a week family element that most households with children get) are taken above the poverty line by that money. Most would be above it anyway while a further 20 per cent are still below the line even with it. [6B]

This does not mean that tax credits are inefficient or wasteful: any household that gets them has a reasonably low income. But it may explain why the jump in the number of recipients when the system was changed in 2003 did not result in a bigger fall in child poverty that year. [6A]

The extent of in-work poverty

Despite the importance of employment in bringing poverty down, employment, even with the help of tax credits, does not guarantee an income above the poverty line: 50 per cent of children in poverty are living in households where someone is doing paid work, most of them in two adult rather than one adult families. [7B]

'All working' households, where at least one person works full-time and any other adult does at least some work, face only a small risk of poverty. The working households most at risk of poverty, though, are those where the only work that is being done is part-time work or where one adult is not working at all. [22A], [22B]

Low pay is of course one of the main reasons why there is so much 'in work' poverty. Five-and-a-half million employees aged 22 and over are paid less than £6.50 per hour. [27A] Part-time work is especially likely to be low paid: 50 per cent of part-time workers earn less than £6.50 an hour [27B], three-quarters of them women. Taking part- and full-time jobs together, two-thirds of all low paid workers are women. [27B]

The two sectors which account for the largest share of low paid employees are the retail and public sectors. [28B] The 30 per cent of low paid employees who work for the public sector does not include those low paid workers employed by contractors working for the public sector.

Although it is not possible to produce a precise figure, probably no more than a fifth of low paid employees work in sectors exposed to international competition. [28B] This means that most low paid workers are low paid because of decisions taken by employers in Britain. The fact that just 15 per cent of workers earning less than £6.50 an hour belong to a trade union must also be a contributory factor. [31B]

Finally, disadvantage at work is a wider issue than 'just' low pay. For example, almost half of men – and a third of women – finding work no longer have that work six months later [30A] and the lower an employee's qualifications, the less likely they are to receive any job-related training. [31A]

The high levels of worklessness among lone parent families

The UK stands out in Europe for the proportion of its children living in workless households. At 17 per cent, the UK rate is 4 per cent higher than the next highest countries (Belgium and Hungary), almost twice that in France and three times that in Denmark. What makes the UK stand out like this is the high number of lone parent households who are workless. [8B]

Over the last decade, the employment rate among lone parents has risen, from around 45 per cent to around 55 per cent. In parallel, the number reliant on social security benefits for two years or more has declined. [5A] However, although the number of children in workless households has come down by about half a million since 1996, most of the fall has been among children in two parent families. [8A]

As a result, whereas most of the children suffering from 'in-work' poverty are in two adult households, most of the children in 'out-of-work' poverty are in lone parent ones. [7B] Despite steady progress, the sheer scale of worklessness among lone parent households means that it remains the principal reason why around half of all children who live with just one of their parents suffer from income poverty.

Where might future reductions in child poverty come from?

However strongly employment grows in future, there is no reason to believe that job growth alone will be able to reduce child poverty by 1.4 million between 2003/04 and 2010 when it has only managed to reduce it by 600,000 since 1998/99. Other policies will be needed too, in particular, regarding:

● low pay, and other conditions at work;
● higher out-of-work benefits.

Low pay is key, not only for in-work poverty but for out-of-work poverty too. This is because pay at the bottom sets a ceiling for out-of-work benefits above which they cannot go if work is still to pay more. The National Minimum Wage is one policy directed at low pay, but its role, important though it is, is to deal with the most extreme cases. In itself the Minimum Wage is still a poverty wage. One avenue that may have the potential to help address in-work poverty is the role of the public sector as an employer. With a quarter of low paid workers employed directly by the public sector, and more working for it indirectly through contractors, standards set here will influence conditions in the private sector too. So far, though, this potential remains unexploited.

There are other things that impact on poverty over which government has direct control. The level of rents in the social housing sector is one. Council Tax is another. In 2003/04, more than half of all households in income poverty, containing 1½ million children, were getting no Council Tax Benefit (CTB) and so were having to pay Council Tax in full. Whereas the issue with CTB as far as pensioners is concerned is the low rate of take-up by those who are entitled to the benefit, [37A] the issue for working-age households in work is the very low level of income at which CTB disappears. This is one aspect of 'in-work' benefit reform that has so far received little attention.

Poverty and work for disabled people
The meaning of disability and its measures
There is no standard way of deciding whether someone is disabled or not, and different surveys use somewhat different definitions. In broad terms, however, there are three types of method:

- Assessment against a list of criteria: a person's mobility, etc. is assessed against a defined set of criteria. This is the approach used in the Family Resources Survey, from which the low income statistics about disabled people in this report are derived.
- Assessment by a doctor: a person's doctor states that, in their view, the person is disabled. This is the approach used in deciding whether or not someone can claim disability benefits, from which the statistics about disabled people in receipt of benefits in this report are derived.
- Self-determination: effectively, the person is asked whether they have a long-term health problem and whether this affects the activities they can undertake or the work they can do. This is the approach used in the General Household Survey, from which the prevalence statistics about disability in this report are derived. It is also the approach used in the Labour Force Survey, from which the work-related statistics about disabled people in this report are derived.

Although these methods are all rather different, one common feature they have is that they all estimate that there are around 5 million adults aged 25 to retirement who are disabled. A second common feature is that they are all using a definition of disability which covers disability arising from mental health as well as from physical health. For example, two-fifths of all claimants of Incapacity Benefit have mental or behaviour disorders.

The meaning of 'lacking but wanting work' and its relationship with disability
The steady and prolonged fall in unemployment is frequently cited as testimony to the success of the Government's economic strategy and its superiority over that of other EU countries where rates of unemployment remain far higher. But the 'unemployed' as they are officially defined and counted are but a part of the group of people who would like a job if one were available. A second, and larger, group is people who want work but fail to meet one of the two criteria required to be considered 'unemployed', namely that they are available to start work in the next two weeks and have been actively seeking work in the last four weeks. Such people are termed 'the economically inactive who want work'.

There are currently around 1^1/2 million people aged 25 to retirement who are 'economically inactive who want work' compared to around 0.8 million 'unemployed'. Furthermore, their numbers have fallen much more slowly than the numbers of 'unemployed': whereas the number 'unemployed' has halved over the last decade, the number who are 'economically inactive but want work' has only fallen by a seventh. [24A]

Importantly, there are around 800,000 disabled people aged 25 to retirement who are 'economically inactive but want work', a figure which is much higher than the 20,000 who are 'unemployed'. In other words, the numbers of disabled adults who lack but want work is five times the number included in the oficial unemployment figures.

The extent of disability and its link with low income
Thirty per cent of working-age disabled adults have incomes that leave them below the poverty line. This rate is higher than it was a decade ago. It is also fully double the rate for working-age adults without a disability. [23A] It is also higher, now, than the rates for either pensioners or children. All of this is crucial

background information for the current review and reform of Incapacity Benefit (IB), the principal benefit that disabled people who are out of work receive.

Working-age disability is widespread and its link to low income clear. Overall, 25 per cent of people aged 45 to 64 suffer either from a disability or a longstanding illness which limits activity. [33A] While people with such conditions are found at every income level, the rate is almost double the average for people in the poorest fifth of the population but only half the average for people in the richest fifth. [33B]

Some 13 per cent of adults aged 25 to retirement are judged to be at risk of developing a mental illness. [34A] Among the poorest fifth of the population, however, the proportion judged to be at risk is, at around 25 per cent, twice the rate for people on average incomes. [34B]

Dependence on social security benefits

Three-quarters of all working-age people who receive one of the key, out-of-work benefits for two years or more are sick or disabled. The number of sick and disabled people in this position has been rising slowly over the last decade and now stands at 2.1 million. [5A] One third are aged 55 to retirement, one third are aged 45 to 54 and one third are aged under 45. [5B]

This growth in long-term dependence on benefits has come about despite the fact that, for someone of working age without dependent children, the value of benefits has declined relative to average income by 20 per cent since the mid-1990s. [4A]

Disability, work and pay

Since the late 1990s, the proportion of people aged 25+ with a work-limiting disability who are either unemployed or 'economically inactive but wanting work', has come down from 25 per cent to 20 per cent. This fall of a fifth is similar to that for people without a work-limiting disability, where it is down from 9 per cent to 7 per cent. [25A] The key question is why this 'lacking but wanting work' rate for disabled people is nearly three times as high as it is for non-disabled people.

The fact that disabled people have lower levels of qualifications on average than non-disabled people is one factor. Limited qualifications increase the risk of not having a job whether disabled or not and the proportion of disabled people with either no qualification or nothing higher than the equivalent of a grade C at GCSE is twice what it is for non-disabled people.

This is, however, not the whole story. First, for any given level of qualification, a disabled person is between two and three times as likely as a non-disabled person to be lacking but wanting work. The additional risk that a disabled person faces is considerable, to such an extent that the 'lacking but wanting work' rate of 14 per cent for a disabled person with higher education is actually higher than the 'lacking but wanting work' rate for a non-disabled person with no qualifications. [25B]

Second, again for any given level of qualification, a disabled person is more likely than a non-disabled person to be low paid. The additional risk of low pay is smaller than the additional risk they face of lacking but wanting work. Nevertheless, that extra risk is there at every level of qualification. [29B] It is also still to be seen after account is taken both of gender and whether the job is full- or part-time. [29A]

The implications for reform of Incapacity Benefit

People with disabilities face many barriers to work: for many, poor qualifications will be one of them and programmes designed to address this are clearly relevant.

However, the finding that at every level of qualifications, disabled people are both more likely to be low paid and more likely to be lacking but wanting work shows that the problem cannot lie solely with disabled people themselves. This is because such a situation – crudely speaking, lower pay and higher 'unemployment' – can only arise if employers perceive disabled employees differently from non-disabled ones. Put another way, and whatever an individual employer's intentions may be, this is evidence that the labour market effectively discriminates against disabled people.

This has two implications for the current reform. First, policies to help disabled people into work, while welcome insofar as many disabled people do want work, will only be of limited success so long as they concentrate on would-be employees alone. Changing employer attitudes is equally important and that is likely to be a long-term task.

Second, however successful reforms may be in helping disabled people into work, millions of people in working-age households will continue to be reliant, long-term, on social security benefits. If poverty rates among this group are not to rise further, never mind begin to fall, 'benefit reform' has to include not just measures to help people get jobs but also substantial increases in the level of benefit.

Other issues

Educational qualifications at 11, 16 and 19+ – and how much they matter

The proportion of 11-year-olds who fail to reach level 4 at Key Stage 2 in both English and maths has continued to come down, albeit much more slowly since 1999 than in the few years before that. [13A] Even so, 40 per cent of children in receipt of free school meals did not reach this level in 2004, twice the rate for other children. [13B]

The proportions of 16-year-olds who got either no GCSEs (6 per cent) or some but fewer than five GCSEs (6 per cent) in 2004 are the same as the proportions in 1998/99. [14A] Three-quarters of 16-year-olds in receipt of free schools meals failed to get five 'good' GCSEs (at grade C or above), one-and-a-half times the rate for other children. [14B]

Nineteen-year-olds whose highest qualification falls short of five 'good' GCSEs or its vocational equivalent (NVQ2) are very unlikely to gain any more qualifications by the time they are 25. By contrast, those who have made this level by age 19 are likely to continue to progress, either academically or vocationally. [16B] The proportion of 19-year-olds failing to reach this critical level has remained stuck at 25 per cent since 1999/2000. [16A]

The economic fortunes of people in their late 20s shows the consequences of reaching different levels of qualification for both work and pay.

- People in their late 20s with no qualifications face a far higher risk than their peers of unemployment: 18 per cent compared with an average of 5 per cent. Anyone possessing at least A-levels or their nearest vocational equivalent (NVQ3) faces a below average risk of being unemployed in their late 20s. [20B]
- By contrast, it is only people with degrees who face a below average risk of still being low paid by their late 20s: 10 per cent compared with an average of 25 per cent. The risk for those with no qualifications is more than 50 per cent. [21B]

Health inequalities

In many areas of health, inequalities are both deep and persistent. For example:

- Babies born to parents from manual backgrounds are 25 per cent more likely to have a low birthweight than those born to parents from non-manual backgrounds. [10A]
- Infant deaths are 50 per cent more likely among those from manual backgrounds than among those from non-manual backgrounds. [11A]
- Death rates from heart disease and lung cancer – the two biggest causes of premature death – for people aged 35 to 64 are around twice as high among those from manual backgrounds as from non-manual backgrounds. [32B]

Crime and its consequences

Crime is an issue for this report because some of the groups of people most likely to suffer from crime are ones who are also most likely to suffer from poverty and exclusion.

The background to this is that the incidence of both burglary and violence with injury are half what they were ten years ago. While the rate of decline has slowed in recent years, both forms of crime are continuing to fall. [44A] Similarly, the number of 18- to 20-year-olds found guilty of an indictable offence is also coming down, by a fifth since 1999. [18A]

Unemployed people are three times as likely as average to be the victims of violent crime. Lone parents are more than twice as likely as average to be burgled. [44B]

It is also the case that households without home contents insurance are three times more likely to be burgled than households with insurance. [47A] Households without this insurance are predominantly poor: 50 per cent of those in the poorest fifth lack such insurance, compared with 10 per cent in the richest fifth. In other words, those who most need its protection are the ones least likely to have it. [47B]

Fear of crime is also greater for people with lower incomes. Among those aged over 60, for example, 36 per cent of women from low income households – and 12 per cent of men – report that they are likely to feel very unsafe out at night, one-and-a-half times the percentage for both men and women over 60 from higher income households. [41B] Furthermore, the proportion who feel very unsafe has not fallen over time. [41A]

Housing quality and availability

Housing will be the subject of its own monitoring report in early 2006 and is thus not covered in detail here. The sharp distinction in fortunes between those who do have housing and those who do not is, however, illustrated by two indicators on central heating and homelessness respectively.

Although poorer households remain more likely to lack central heating, the proportion who do so is now actually less than that for households on average incomes five years ago, having halved over the last decade. [48A]

By contrast, the number of people accepted by their local authority as homeless has risen by 20 per cent over the same period and now stands at around 200,000 households each year. Just about all of this rise has been among households without dependent children, who now constitute two-thirds of the total. [49A]

Geographical patterns

The key features of the four maps for Great Britain and four maps for England include:

- The pattern of dependence on social security benefits among working-age people is largely similar to the pattern of dependence among pensioners, with urban, rural and coastal areas all figuring in the list of the most dependent. [GB1], [GB2]
- Low pay is most widespread in rural parts of England, mid- and west-Wales, and southern Scotland. London, the northern cities and Glasgow/Edinburgh all have below average proportions of low pay. [GB3]
- Every part of Scotland has rates of premature death above the GB average. Elsewhere, rates are highest in the inner cities and parts of South Wales. [GB4]
- Both failure to obtain five or more GCSEs and underage pregnancies are most common in urban areas and, with some exceptions, follow similar patterns. [E1], [E2]
- The local authorities who help the fewest of their older citizens to live at home are outside of the cities, across southern England, East Anglia and Yorkshire. [E3]
- Though worst in London and the North East, both rural and urban areas anywhere in the country can have serious problems of homelessness. [E4]

Summary of the poverty and social exclusion indicators

Indicator	Trends over time	
	Over the medium term	Over latest year of available data
Low income		
1 Numbers in low income	Improved	Improved
2 Low income by age group	Mixed	Mixed
3 Low income by family type	Improved	Mixed
4 Out-of-work benefit levels	Mixed	Mixed
5 Long-term recipients of out-of-work benefits	Steady	Steady
6 In receipt of tax credits	n/a	n/a
Children		
7 In low income households	Improved	Improved
8 In workless households	Improved	Improved
9 Concentrations of poor children	Steady	Steady
10 Low birthweight babies	Worsened	Steady
11 Child health and well-being	Steady	Steady
12 Underage pregnancies	Steady	Steady
13 Low attainment at school (11-year-olds)	Improved	Improved
14 Low attainment at school (16-year-olds)	Steady	Steady
15 School exclusions	Worsened	Worsened
Young adults		
16 Without a basic qualification	Steady	Steady
17 School leavers	Steady	Steady
18 With a criminal record	Improved	Improved
19 In low income households	Steady	Steady
20 Unemployment	Steady	Steady
21 Low pay	Steady	Steady
Working-age adults aged 25+		
22 Low income and work	Worsened	Mixed
23 Low income and disability	Steady	Steady
24 Wanting paid work	Improved	Steady
25 Work and disability	Improved	Improved
26 Workless households	Steady	Steady
27 Low pay by gender	Steady	Improved
28 Low pay by industry	n/a	n/a
29 Low pay and disability	n/a	n/a
30 Insecure at work	Steady	Steady
31 Support at work	Improved	Steady
32 Premature death	Improved	Improved
33 Limiting longstanding illness	Steady	Improved
34 Mental health	Steady	Improved

Indicator	Trends over time	
	Over the medium term	*Over latest year of available data*
Pensioners		
35 In low income households	Improved	Improved
36 No private income	Improved	Steady
37 Non-take-up of benefits	Worsened	Steady
38 Excess winter deaths	Steady	Steady
39 Limiting longstanding illness	Steady	Improved
40 Help to live at home	Worsened	Worsened
41 Anxiety	Steady	Improved
Communities		
42 Polarisation of low income	Improved	Improved
43 Concentrations of low income	n/a	n/a
44 Victims of crime	Improved	Improved
45 Transport	Steady	Steady
46 Without a bank account	Improved	Improved
47 Without home contents insurance	Improved	Improved
48 Without central heating	Improved	Improved
49 Homelessness	Worsened	Improved
50 In mortgage arrears	Improved	Improved

Summary of regional differences

Key: + Better than the national average; = Around the national average; – Worse than the national average; N/A Indicator not analysed for the region in question

Indicator	East	East Midlands	London	North East	North West	Northern Ireland	Scotland	South East	South West	Wales	West Midlands	Yorkshire and the Humber
Low income												
1 Numbers in low income	+	=	–	=	=	n/a	=	+	=	=	=	=
Children												
7 In low income households	+	=	–	=	=	=	=	+	=	=	=	=
8 In workless households	+	=	–	–	=	=	=	+	+	=	=	=
10 Low birthweight babies	+	=	–	=	=	n/a	=	+	+	=	–	=
11a Infant mortality	+	=	=	=	=	n/a	=	+	+	=	–	=
11b Dental ill-health	+	=	+	=	=	n/a	–	+	=	=	+	–
12 Underage pregnancies	+	=	=	–	=	n/a	=	+	+	=	=	–
13 Low attainment at school (11-year-olds)	=	=	+	=	=	n/a	n/a	=	=	+	=	–
14 Low attainment at school (16-year-olds)	+	=	+	–	–	n/a	n/a	=	=	+	=	–
15 School exclusions	=	=	=	=	–	n/a	+	=	=	+	=	=
Young adults												
16 Without a basic qualification	=	=	=	–	–	+	+	=	=	=	–	=
17 School leavers	=	=	=	=	=	n/a	n/a	=	=	n/a	=	=
20 Unemployment	=	=	–	–	=	=	=	+	=	=	=	=
Working-age adults aged 25+												
24 Wanting paid work	+	=	–	=	=	+	–	=	+	=	=	=
25 Work and disability	=	=	=	=	=	+	=	=	=	–	=	=
27 Low pay by gender	=	–	+	=	–	+	+	+	+	=	=	=
32 Premature death	+	=	=	–	–	n/a	–	+	+	=	=	=
33 Limiting longstanding illness	+	=	+	–	–	–	–	+	=	=	=	=
34 Mental health	+	=	=	=	=	n/a	n/a	=	=	n/a	=	=
Pensioners												
35 In low income households	=	–	–	+	=	n/a	+	+	=	=	–	=
38 Excess winter deaths	=	=	=	+	=	n/a	+	=	=	=	=	=
39 Limiting longstanding illness	+	=	=	–	–	–	=	+	+	–	=	=
40 Help to live at home	–	=	=	+	=	n/a	n/a	–	–	+	=	=
Communities												
44 Victims of crime	+	=	–	=	–	n/a	n/a	=	=	+	–	–
48 Without central heating	+	=	=	+	–	+	=	=	=	=	=	–
49 Homelessness	+	=	–	–	=	n/a	n/a	+	+	n/a	=	=

1 Low income

This chapter has two themes containing six indicators. The themes are:

● trends in low income;
● in receipt of state benefits.

Further indicators on low income also appear at the start of each of the other five chapters.

Trends in low income
Choice of indicators
This theme provides a range of statistics on both the number and percentage of people with low income, usually since 1994/95, but in one case going back to 1979.

The principal measure of low income is a household income that is 60 per cent or less of the contemporary average (median) household income. In the most recent year, 2003/04, that threshold, adjusted for the number of people living in the household, was worth:

● £180 per week for a two adult household;
● £100 per week for a single adult;
● £260 per week for two adults living with two children;
● £180 per week for a single adult living with two children.

This sum of money applies after income tax and national insurance have been deducted from earnings and after council tax, rent, mortgage and water charges have been paid.

The first graph of the first indicator shows how the number of people living in households below this threshold has changed over time. As well as this relative measure, it also shows the number of people living below a fixed income threshold, namely 60 per cent of average household income in 1996/97, adjusted when comparing other years only for price inflation. The supporting graph shows how the proportion of people in the poorest fifth of the population varies by region, comparing these proportions with the equivalent proportions for the richest fifth.

The second indicator provides an analysis by age group. The first graph shows the risk of a person being in a low income household, with the data shown separately for children, pensioners and working-age adults without dependent children. The supporting graph provides a breakdown of the people in low income households by age group.

The third indicator provides further information on the age groups in low income households. Because the trends are somewhat different when considered in terms of absolute numbers rather than percentage risks, the first graph of this indicator shows the numbers of people in low income households by type of person (children, pensioners and working-age adults with or without dependent children) and type of household (single adult or couple), with the specific data showing the change in the numbers between 1998/98 and 2003/04. The supporting graph shows how the people living in low income households where the household is paying full Council Tax divide by age group, Council Tax being one of the taxes that hits many low income households the hardest.

What the indicators show

Indicator 1 Numbers in low income

The number of people in relative low income is now lower than at any time since 1987, but is still much higher than in the early 1980s.

Inner London is deeply divided: it has by far the highest proportion of people on a low income but also the highest proportion of people on a high income.

Indicator 2 Low income by age group

The proportion of children and pensioners who live in low income households has been falling. In contrast, the proportion for working-age adults without dependent children has remained broadly unchanged.

A third of all people in low income households are working-age adults without dependent children.

Indicator 3 Low income by family type

The only group where the number of low income people is increasing is working-age adults without dependent children.

One-and-a-half million children in England and Wales are living in low income households where the household is paying full Council Tax.

In receipt of state benefits

Choice of indicators

This theme provides statistics on both the number of recipients of certain benefits and the value of some of those benefits. Benefit recipient numbers are shown for long-term (two years or more) out-of-work benefits as well as for in-work tax credits (and their predecessors).

The first graph of the first indicator shows how the value of Income Support has varied over time for selected family types. The supporting graph provides a breakdown of out-of-work benefit recipients by age group.

The second indicator shows how the number of working-age people in receipt of out-of-work benefit for two years or more has changed over time, with the data broken down by type of claimant. The majority of long-term claimants of out-of-work benefits are sick or disabled and, in this context, the supporting graph provides an age breakdown of those who have either been in receipt of Incapacity Benefit for two years or more or are in receipt of Severe Disablement Allowance.

In April 2003, the Working Tax Credit and Child Tax Credit replaced the Working Families Tax Credit (WFTC) and Disabled Person's Tax Credit (DPTC). These, in turn, had been introduced in 1999 to replace Family Credit (FC) and Disability Working Allowance (DWA). The final indicator shows how, on a like-for-like basis, the number of people in receipt of tax credits has changed over time. The supporting graph provides an analysis of the people in households in receipt of tax credits over and above the basic family element, with the three categorisations being according to whether or not the household income is below 60 per cent of median income after deducting housing costs and whether or not it would have been if no tax credits has been received.

What the indicators show
Indicator 4 Out-of-work benefit levels
The level of Income Support for both pensioners and families with two or more children has gone up much faster than average earnings in recent years, but that for working-age adults without children has fallen considerably behind.

Among all adults, almost half of those reliant on state benefits are of working age and do not have dependent children.

Indicator 5 Long-term working-age recipients of out-of-work benefits
Three-quarters of working-age people receiving a key out-of-work benefit for two years or more are now sick or disabled.

Two-thirds of the long-term claimants of Incapacity Benefit or Severe Disablement Allowance are aged less than 55 and a third are aged less than 45.

Indicator 6 In receipt of tax credits
The introduction of Working and Child Tax Credits means that the number of working households who are in receipt of in-work benefits has more than trebled since 1996.

Only a fifth of tax credit recipients are no longer in low income because of the tax credit monies received.

Relevant Public Service Agreement 2004 targets

What	Who
Halve the number of children in relative low-income households between 1998/99 and 2010/11, on the way to eradicating child poverty by 2020, including:	DWP and HM Treasury
• reducing the proportion of children in workless households by 5% between spring 2005 and spring 2008; and • increasing the proportion of parents with care on Income Support and income-based Jobseeker's Allowance who receive maintenance for their children by 65% by March 2008.	
By 2008, be paying Pension Credit to at least 3.2 million pensioner households, while maintaining a focus on the most disadvantaged by ensuring that at least 2.2 million of these households are in receipt of the Guarantee Credit.	DWP

Selected major initiatives under way

Policy	Starting dates	Key department	Key delivery agency	Budget/target/comment
National Minimum Wage	April 1999: introduced October 2000: uprated October 2001: uprated October 2002: uprated October 2003: uprated October 2004: uprated October 2005: uprated	DTI	HM Revenue & Customs and employers	When first introduced, set at £3.60 per hour for those aged 22 years and over, unless in an exempt category or on a registered training scheme (in which case only £3.20). £3.00 per hour for those aged 18-21. For those aged 22 and over, raised to £3.70 in October 2000, £4.10 in October 2001, £4.20 in October 2002, £4.50 in October 2003, £4.85 in October 2004 and £5.05 in October 2005, with a further uprating to £5.35 in October 2006. For those aged 18 to 21, raised to £3.20 in October 2000, £3.50 in October 2001, £3.60 in October 2002, £3.80 in October 2003, £4.10 in October 2004 and £4.25 in October 2005, with a further uprating to £4.45 in October 2006. Introduced for the first time for those aged 16 to 17 in October 2004, at £3.00. The Low Pay Commission estimated that the original National Minimum Wage affected 1.3 million jobs, rising to 1.5m after the 2001 and 2002 increases.
Working Families Tax Credit (WFTC) (replaced Family Credit)	October 1999: introduced October 2000: uprated April 2001: uprated October 2001: uprated April 2002: uprated June 2002: uprated October 2002: uprated April 2003: replaced by a combination of Working Tax Credit and Child Tax Credit	HM Treasury and DWP	HM Revenue & Customs and employers	The level of the credit is dependent on the number of children, how many hours worked (the minimum is 16 hours), childcare costs and levels of savings. When first introduced, guaranteed a weekly gross income of £200 for a family with one full-time worker. No tax until £235 per week for families with one full-timer (55p taper, down from 70p under the Family Credit scheme that it replaced). Minimum income guarantee raised to £208 in October 2000, £214 in April 2001, £225 in October 2001, £227 in April 2002, £230 in June 2002 and £237 in October 2002. Only available to those with savings of less than £8,000, with decreased eligibility for those with savings between £3,000 and £8,000, implying total expenditure of around £6 billion.

Policy	Starting dates	Key department	Key delivery agency	Budget/target/comment
Children's Tax Credit (replaced Married Couples' Allowance)	April 2001: introduced April 2003: replaced by the Child Tax Credit	HM Treasury and DWP	HM Revenue & Customs and employers	Included a childcare allowance of up to 70% of childcare costs for working parents, up to a limit of £100 for one child and £150 for 2+ children (from October 1999) and £135 for one child and £200 for 2+ children (from April 2001). In its final year (2002), Working Families Tax Credit paid an average of £86 a week to 1.4 million households. Payable to anyone paying tax who has a child aged 16 or under (implemented as a reduction in the tax bill of the claimant). Maximum tax reduction of £529 per annum. This compares with £197 for the Married Couples' Allowance which it replaced. Maximum amount for the family element given to those on an annual income of £32,750 or less. For every £15 above this, £1 deducted.
Disabled Persons Tax Credit (replaced Disability Working Allowance)	October 1999: introduced April 2001: uprated October 2001: uprated April 2002: uprated June 2002: uprated October 2002: uprated April 2003: replaced by the Working Tax Credit	HM Treasury and DWP	HM Revenue & Customs and employers	Originally guaranteed a weekly income of £231 for a couple with one child. Minimum income guarantee raised to £246 in April 2001, £260 in April 2002, £263 in June 2002 and £264 in October 2002. Operated like the Working Families Tax Credit, except no children required to be eligible.
Increase in Child Allowance within Income Support	November 1998: uprated October 1999: uprated April 2000: uprated October 2000: uprated April 2002: uprated April 2003: replaced by the Child Tax Credit	DWP	Jobcentre Plus	Raised by £2.50 per week in November 1998, by a further £4.70 per week in October 1999, by a further £1.10 per week in April 2000, by a further £4.35 per week in October 2000, and by a further £3.50 per week in April 2002.
Working Tax Credit (replaced Working Families Tax Credit and Disabled Persons Tax Credit)	April 2003: introduced April 2004: uprated April 2005: uprated	HM Treasury	HM Revenue & Customs and employers	Increases the level of tax credits for people with dependent children and extends them to some people without dependent children. Three types of family are eligible: a) Households with dependent children where at least one partner works at least 16 hours per week (maximum of £75 per week if working at least 30 hours and £62 if working 16-29 hours). b) Households without dependent children where at least one partner is aged 25 or over and works at least 30 hours per week (maximum of £75 per week if a couple and £44 per week if single). c) Workers with a disability who work at least 16 hours per week (maximum as per the other family types plus up to £42 for the disability). Subject to eligibility, the maximum is available for households with an average weekly income of up to around £100. For each £1 above this level, the amount reduces by 37 pence. So, some Working Tax Credit will be available up to weekly incomes of around £300.

Policy	Starting dates	Key department	Key delivery agency	Budget/target/comment
				Includes an additional component to help cover the costs of childcare for those households where all partners work at least 16 hours per week (up to 70% of the costs paid up to a maximum amount – £175 for one child and £300 for 2+ children for 2005/06). Savings are not taken into consideration.
Child Tax Credit (replaced Children's Tax Credit and Child Allowance within Income Support)	April 2003: introduced April 2004: uprated April 2005: uprated	HM Treasury	HM Revenue & Customs and employers	Replaced the Children's Tax Credit and the child-related part of the Working Families Tax Credit. Also replaced the child elements of Income Support and Job Seeker's Allowance. Subject to a means test, available to any household with dependent children (up to age 19 if child in full-time education), whether or not anyone in the household is working. The maximum credit available depends upon the number and age of the children in the household, but is around £10 per week plus £33 for each dependent child. So, for example, the maximum available to a family with two adults and two children both over the age of one is £72 per week. Such a family would be entitled to this maximum with an average weekly income of anything up to around £300. Above this level, the credit reduces by 37 pence for every extra £1 in income until all but £10 of it has disappeared (at a weekly income of around £450). The remaining £10 a week 'family' element remains undiminished until household income exceeds around £1,000 per week.
Increases in Child Benefit	April 1999: uprated April 2000: uprated April 2001: uprated April 2002: uprated April 2003: uprated April 2004: uprated April 2005: uprated	HM Treasury	Child Benefits Agency	Raised to £14.40 for the eldest child in April 1999, to £15 in April 2000, to £15.50 in April 2001, to £15.75 in April 2002, to £16.05 in April 2003, to £16.50 in April 2004 and to £17.00 in April 2005. Similar proportional rises for other children from £9.30 prior to April 1999 to £11.40 in April 2005.
Pensioners' Minimum Income Guarantee (MIG)	April 1999: introduced April 2000: uprated April 2001: uprated April 2002: uprated October 2003: replaced by Pension Credit	DWP	Pension Service	When introduced, set at £75 a week for single pensioners and £116.60 for pensioner couples, representing increases of around £4 and £7 respectively over the levels of income support that were previously available. For single pensioners, raised to £78.45 in April 2000, £92.15 in April 2001, £98.15 in April 2002 and £102.10 in April 2003. For pensioner couples, raised to £121.95 in April 2000, £140.55 in April 2001, £149.80 in April 2002 and £155.80 in April 2003. Budget estimated at £3.8 billion for 1999/00, £4.1 billion for 2000/01, and £4.4 billion for 2002/03.
Pension Credit (replaced the Minimum Income Guarantee)	October 2003: introduced October 2004: uprated April 2005: uprated	DWP	Pension Service	The main change from the Minimum Income Guarantee that it replaced is that the Pension Credit will operate like the other tax credits, with a reduction of 40 pence for every additional £1 in pension income. In contrast, the Minimum Income Guarantee was a fixed guaranteed minimum income, with the individual losing a full £1 in government benefit for every £1 that their pension income was above this level.

Policy	Starting dates	Key department	Key delivery agency	Budget/target/comment
				When first introduced, the guaranteed minimum weekly income was the same as for the Minimum Income Guarantee, namely £102.10 for a single pensioner and £155.80 for a pensioner couple. Uprated to £105.45 and £160.95 in October 2004 and to £109.45 and £167.05 in April 2005. Depends on household, rather than individual, income. The basic State Retirement Pension is £82 for a single pensioner and £131 for a pensioner couple. So, for someone with the full State Retirement Pension, the maximum amount of Pension Credit is around £27 for a single pensioner and £36 for a pensioner couple. $2^{1}/_{2}$ million households receiving the Pension Credit in July 2004. A target of at least 3 million households by 2006, and 3.2 million by 2008. Estimated cost of the reform, including changes to Housing Benefit and Council Tax Benefit for pensioners, estimated at around £1 billion in 2003/04 and £2 billion in 2004/05.
Second State Pension	April 2002: introduced	DWP	Pension Service	An extension to SERPS and aims to increase the income provided by SERPS for those on low incomes. Those earning less than £12,100 have their pension calculated as though their earnings were actually £12,100.

Numbers in low income

Indicator
1

The number of people in relative low income is now lower than at any time since 1987, but is still much higher than in the early 1980s.

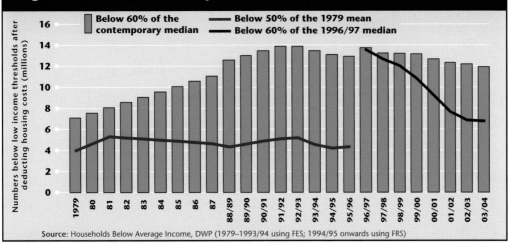

Below 60% of the contemporary median
Below 50% of the 1979 mean
Below 60% of the 1996/97 median

Source: Households Below Average Income, DWP (1979–1993/94 using FES; 1994/95 onwards using FRS)

Inner London is deeply divided: it has by far the highest proportion of people on a low income but also the highest proportion of people on a high income.

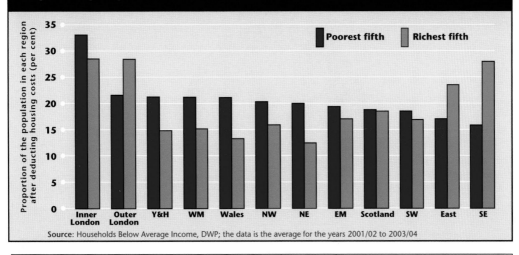

Poorest fifth   Richest fifth

Source: Households Below Average Income, DWP; the data is the average for the years 2001/02 to 2003/04

The first graph provides three measures of low income. The bars shows the number of people below 60% of contemporary median income for each year since 1979. The line from 1996/97 onwards shows the number of people below a fixed threshold of 60% of 1996/97 median income (adjusted for price inflation) – the 1996/97 threshold has been chosen as it is one of the thresholds used by the government. The line from 1979 to 1994/95 shows the number of people below a fixed threshold of 50% of 1979 mean income (adjusted for price inflation) – 50% of mean rather than 60% of median is used because this was the threshold of low income commonly used at the time.

Note that data for 1980, 1982 to 1986 and 1998/90 is not available and thus the figures on the two graphs for these years have each been interpolated from the previous and subsequent year figures.

The second graph shows the proportion of the population whose income is in the lowest and highest income quintiles (fifths) in each region in Great Britain. Inner and Outer London are presented separately as the results are so different. To improve statistical reliability, the data is averaged for the years 2001/02 to 2003/04.

The data source for both graphs is Households Below Average Income, based on the Family Resources Survey (FRS) since 1994/95 and the Family Expenditure Survey (FES) for earlier years. The data relates to Great Britain. The self-employed are included in the statistics. Income is disposable household income after housing costs. All data is equivalised (adjusted) to account for variation in household size and composition.

Overall adequacy of the indicator: **high**. The FRS and FES are both well-established annual government surveys, designed to be representative of the population as a whole.

Low income by age group

The proportion of children and pensioners who live in low income households has been falling. In contrast, the proportion for working-age adults without dependent children has remained broadly unchanged.

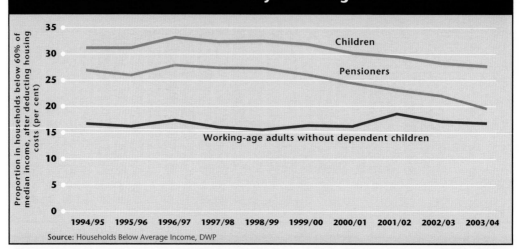

Source: Households Below Average Income, DWP

A third of all people in low income households are working-age adults without dependent children.

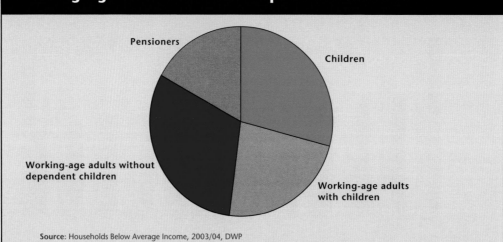

Source: Households Below Average Income, 2003/04, DWP

The first graph shows the risk of a person being in a low income household, with the data shown separately for children, pensioners and working-age adults without dependent children. For presentational reasons, the figures for working-age adults with dependent children (which broadly follow the same trends as for children themselves) are not shown.

The second graph shows a breakdown of the people in low income households according to whether they are children, pensioners, working-age adults with dependent children or working-age adults without dependent children.

The data source for both graphs is Households Below Average Income, based on the Family Resources Survey (FRS). The data relates to Great Britain. The self-employed are included in the statistics. Income is disposable household income after housing costs. All data is equivalised (adjusted) to account for variation in household size and composition.

Overall adequacy of the indicator: **high**. The FRS is a well-established annual government survey, designed to be representative of the population as a whole.

Low income by family type

Indicator
3

The only group where the number of low income people is increasing is working-age adults without dependent children.

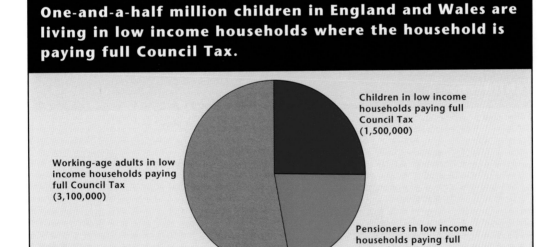

Change in the number of people below 60% of contemporary median income after deducting housing costs between 1998/99 and 2003/04 (thousands)

- Single adult households
- Couple households

| Pensioners | Children | Working-age adults with children | Working-age adults without dependent children |

Source: Households Below Average Income, DWP

One-and-a-half million children in England and Wales are living in low income households where the household is paying full Council Tax.

Children in low income households paying full Council Tax (1,500,000)

Working-age adults in low income households paying full Council Tax (3,100,000)

Pensioners in low income households paying full Council Tax (1,300,000)

Source: Households Below Average Income, DWP; the data is the average for 2001/02 to 2003/04

The first graph shows the numbers of people in low income households by type of person (children, pensioners and working-age adults with or without dependent children) and type of household (single adult or couple), with the specific data showing the change in the numbers between 1998/99 and 2003/04.

The second graph shows the people living in low income households where the household is paying full Council Tax by age group. To improve statistical reliability, the data is the average for the three years from 2001/02 to 2003/04.

The data source for both graphs is Households Below Average Income, based on the Family Resources Survey (FRS). The data in the first graph relates to Great Britain and the data in the second graph relates to England and Wales (in Scotland, Council Tax and water charges are paid as part of the same bill so it is not possible to distinguish people who are paying no Council Tax). The self-employed are included in the statistics. Income is disposable household income after housing costs. All data is equivalised (adjusted) to account for variation in household size and composition.

Overall adequacy of the indicator: **high**. The FRS is a well-established annual government survey, designed to be representative of the population as a whole.

Out-of-work benefit levels

The level of Income Support for both pensioners and families with two or more children has gone up much faster than average earnings in recent years, but for working-age adults without children it has fallen considerably behind.

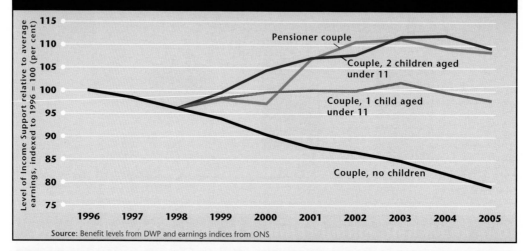

Source: Benefit levels from DWP and earnings indices from ONS

Among all adults, almost half of those reliant on state benefits are of working age and do not have dependent children.

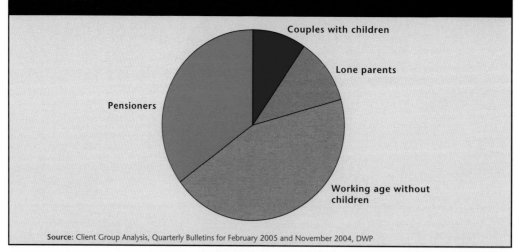

Source: Client Group Analysis, Quarterly Bulletins for February 2005 and November 2004, DWP

The first graph shows how the value of Income Support has varied over time for selected family types. The selected family types are pensioner couples, couples with two children aged less than 11, couples with one child aged less than 11 and couples with no children. In each case, the base year is 1996, at which point the value of the benefits is set to 100%. The figures are deflated by the growth in average earnings in each year.

The data source for the earnings data is the ONS Average Earnings Index, using the series which is seasonally adjusted. The family types were selected to best illustrate the differing trends over time. So, for example, single adults with no dependent children is not shown as it has followed similar trends to that for couples with no dependent children. No disability benefits have been included.

The second graph provides a breakdown of the recipients of key benefits. 'Key benefits' is a DWP term which covers the following benefits: Jobseeker's Allowance, Income Support, Incapacity Benefit, Severe Disablement Allowance, Disability Living Allowance and Pension Credit.

The data source is the various Client Group Analysis publications of the DWP. The working-age data is for February 2005 and the pensioner data is for November 2004. The data relates to Great Britain.

Overall adequacy of the indicator: **high**. The statistics in the first graph are factual and those in the second graph are considered to be very reliable.

Long-term working-age recipients of out-of-work benefits

Indicator 5

Three-quarters of working-age people receiving a key out-of-work benefit for two years or more are now sick or disabled.

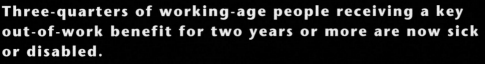

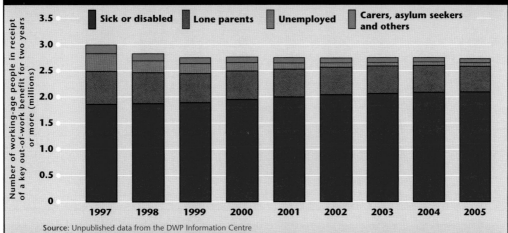

Source: Unpublished data from the DWP Information Centre

Two-thirds of the long-term claimants of Incapacity Benefit or Severe Disablement Allowance are aged less than 55 and a third are aged less than 45.

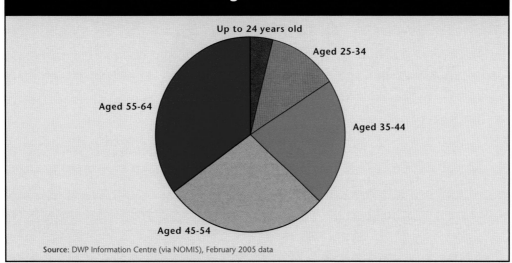

Source: DWP Information Centre (via NOMIS), February 2005 data

The first graph shows all those of working age who were in receipt of a key out-of-work benefit for two years or more. 'Key out-of-work benefit' is a DWP term which covers the following benefits: Jobseeker's Allowance, Income Support, Incapacity Benefit and Severe Disablement Allowance. Note that this list is slightly different from 'key benefits', which also include Disability Living Allowance. For each year, the total is broken down by type of claimant: unemployed, sick and disabled, lone parents and others (eg carers and asylum seekers).

The second graph shows, for the latest year, an age breakdown for those who have either been in receipt of Incapacity Benefit for two years or more or are in receipt of Severe Disablement Allowance.

The data source for both graphs is the DWP Information Centre, with the data obtained via NOMIS. The data relates to Great Britain and is for the month of February in each year. The data has been analysed to avoid double-counting of those receiving multiple benefits by matching data from individual samples.

Overall adequacy of the indicator: **high**. The data is thought to be very reliable. It is based on information collected by the DWP for the administration of benefits.

In receipt of tax credits

Indicator
6

The introduction of Working and Child Tax Credits means that the number of working households who are in receipt of in-work benefits has more than trebled since 1996.

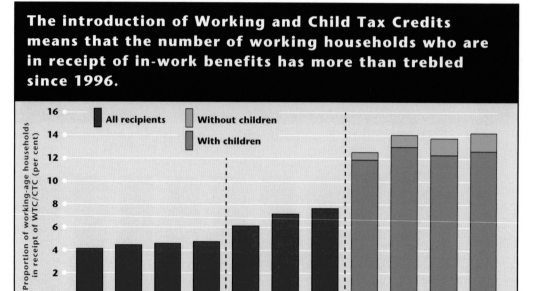

Source: Information Analysis Directorate, DWP (to 1999); Geographic analyses, HM Revenue & Customs (2000 onwards)

Only a fifth of tax credit recipients are no longer in low income because of the tax credit monies received.

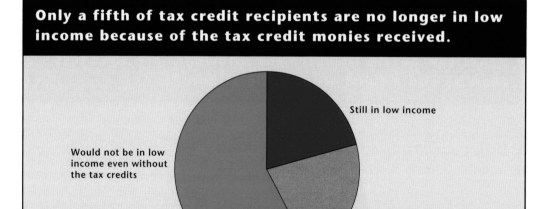

Source: Households Below Average Income 2003/04, DWP

In April 2003, the Working Tax Credit (WTC) and Child Tax Credit (CTC) replaced the Working Families Tax Credit (WFTC) and Disabled Person's Tax Credit (DPTC). These, in turn, had been introduced in 1999 to replace Family Credit (FC) and Disability Working Allowance (DWA).

The first graph shows the proportion of working-age households in receipt of tax credits (and their equivalents in previous years) for each year since 1996. Care has been taken to ensure that the data is on a like-for-like basis. In particular: the 2003 to 2005 data is total recipients of either WTC or CTC in the stated month excluding those just receiving the family element of CTC; the 2001 and 2002 data is total recipients of either WFTC or DPTC in the stated month; and the 1996 to 1999 data is total recipients of either FC or DWA in the stated month. The data relates to Great Britain and its sources are The Department for Work and Pensions Information Centre for data on FC and DWA and HM Revenue & Customs for data on WTC, CTC, WFTC and DPTC.

The second graph provides an analysis of the people in households in receipt of tax credits over and above the basic family element of CTC, with the three categorisations being according to whether or not the household income is below 60% of median income after deducting housing costs and whether or not it would have been if no tax credits has been received. The data source is Households Below Average Income, based on the Family Resources Survey (FRS). The data relates to Great Britain and is for the year 2003/04.

Overall adequacy of the indicator: *medium*. All the data is considered to be very reliable and provides an accurate count of the people on those benefit/tax credits. However, the extensive changes in the system from year-to-year makes the data somewhat difficult to interpret.

2 Children

This chapter has three themes containing nine indicators. The themes are:

- economic circumstances;
- health and well-being;
- education.

Economic circumstances
Choice of indicators
The indicators provide three complementary views of the situation for children in low income households.

The first indicator provides more information over time both on the number of children in low income households, going back to 1979, and on the government's child poverty targets. The supporting graph shows these children's family and work circumstances.

The second indicator shows the number of children in workless households since 1996, and according to whether they are living with one parent or two. The supporting graph shows how the UK compares with all other EU member states.

The third indicator shows how children entitled to free school meals (that is, in low income households without work) are concentrated in certain schools and how, in turn, this affects their overall perception of how many poor children there are overall.

What the indicators show
Indicator 7 In low income households
The number of children in low income households has fallen by $3/4$ million since 1996/97 and currently stands at $3^1/2$ million. Children remain more likely than adults to live in low income households.

Two-fifths of the children in low income households live in couple households where at least one of the adults is in paid work.

Indicator 8 In workless households
The number of children in workless households has fallen by a quarter over the last decade, with most of this fall being for children in couple households.

The UK has a higher proportion of its children living in workless households than any other EU country.

Indicator 9 Concentrations of poor children
Half of all the primary school children who are eligible for free school meals are concentrated in a fifth of the schools, a similar proportion to a decade ago.

Pupils eligible for free school meals have, on average, twice as many pupils in their school eligible for free school meals.

Health and well-being
Choice of indicators
These indicators cover birthweight, infant death and underage pregnancy. They show the ten-year trends and how both the trends and the levels differ according to social class.

Two of the three supporting graphs show how the incidence of the particular problems varies either by family or work status. The third supporting graph is on the subject of 5-year olds' dental health.

What the indicators show
Indicator 10 Low birthweight babies
Babies born to parents from manual social backgrounds continue to be more likely to be of low birthweight than those born to parents from non-manual social backgrounds.

Babies born to lone parents are more likely to be of low birthweight than babies born to couples.

Indicator 11 Child health and well-being
While the rate of infant deaths amongst those from non-manual social backgrounds has fallen over the last decade, the pattern for those from manual social backgrounds is less clear.

Five-year-olds in Wales and Scotland have, on average, more than twice as many missing, decayed or filled teeth as five-year-olds in the West Midlands and South East of England.

Indicator 12 Underage pregnancies
While the number of births to girls conceiving under age 16 has fallen by a quarter since 1996, the total number of conceptions has remained unchanged because of an increased number of abortions.

Teenage motherhood is seven times as common amongst those from manual social backgrounds as for those from professional backgrounds.

Education
Choice of indicators
Two of the three indicators under this theme show the progress there has been since the mid-1990s in the number of children reaching certain minimum educational standards. For 11-year-olds, the standard is Level 4 at Key Stage 2 in each of maths and English. For 16-year-olds, the standards are first, at least one GCSE and second, at least five GCSEs.

The graph for the 11-year-olds also shows the results separately for schools containing a high proportion of children with low incomes. The supporting graphs take the comparison between poor children and other children further, showing the results separately for boys and girls according to whether they get free school meals. Perforce, the GCSE standard being measured here is the higher one of at least five GCSEs at grade C or above.

The third graph shows the number of children permanently excluded from school in each year since the mid-1990s, separately for England, Wales and Scotland. The supporting graph, which also has a time dimension to it, categorises exclusions according to the ethnicity of the child.

What the indicators show

Indicator 13 Low attainment at school (11-year-olds)

Progress continues to be made in the literacy and numeracy of 11-year-olds – including those in deprived schools – but the rate of progress has slowed in recent years.

Eleven-year-old pupils in receipt of free school meals are twice as likely not to achieve basic standards in literacy and numeracy as other eleven-year-old pupils.

Indicator 14 Low attainment at school (16-year-olds)

Twelve per cent of 16-year-olds still obtain fewer than five GCSEs and 6 per cent get no GCSEs at all, both figures being unchanged since 1998/99.

Three-quarters of pupils in receipt of free school meals do not obtain five or more GCSEs at grade C or above. This compares with less than half of other pupils.

Indicator 15 School exclusions

The number of permanent exclusions has been increasing since 1999.

The rate of permanent exclusions of Black Caribbean pupils has halved in recent years, but they are still three times as likely to be excluded as White pupils.

Economic circumstances
Relevant Public Service Agreement 2004 targets

What	Who
Halve the number of children in relative low-income households between 1998/99 and 2010/11, on the way to eradicating child poverty by 2020, including:	DWP and HM Treasury
• reducing the proportion of children in workless households by 5% between spring 2005 and spring 2008; and • increasing the proportion of parents with care on Income Support and income-based Jobseeker's Allowance who receive maintenance for their children by 65% by March 2008.	
As a contribution to reducing the proportion of children living in households where no-one is working by 2008:	DWP and DfES
• increase the stock of Ofsted-registered childcare by 10%; • increase the take-up of formal childcare by lower income working families by 50%; and • introduce a successful light-touch childcare approval scheme by April 2005.	

Selected major initiatives under way (Also see the Low Income chapter.)

Policy	Starting dates	Key department	Key delivery agency	Budget/target/comment
National childcare strategy	1998: launched	DfES	Local authorities	Updated in 2004 as part The Five Year Strategy for Children and Learners. Aims to provide access to affordable childcare and early years services, supporting child development, removing barriers to parental employment and alleviating child poverty. Targets: 1. Two million new childcare places by 2006, with 1.8 million having been achieved by 2004. 2. 2,500 Children's Centres by 2008, including a centre in each of the 20% most disadvantaged wards in England. 3. A budget of around £400 million each year from 2001/02 to 2003/04. Additional resources of £770 million by 2007/08 compared with 2004/05.

Health and well-being
Relevant Public Service Agreement 2004 targets

What	Who
Reduce the under-18 conception rate by 50% by 2010 as part of a broader strategy to improve sexual health.	DfES and DH
Reduce health inequalities by 10% by 2010 as measured by mortality and life expectancy	DH

Selected major initiatives under way

Policy	Starting dates	Key department	Key delivery agency	Budget/target/comment
Sure Start	June 1999: introduced	Sure Start Unit	Local authorities, voluntary sector, NHS and government regional offices	Aims: to increase the availability of childcare for all children; to improve health, education and emotional development for young children; and to support parents in their role and in developing their employment aspirations. By May 2003, around 500 Sure Start programmes were in action, reaching up to one third of under-fours living in poverty. Budget of £450 million for 1999/2000 to 2001/02, and a further £580 million for the period to 2004.
Sure Start Maternity Grant	March 2000: introduced (replacing maternity payment scheme) Autumn 2000: uprated April 2002: uprated	DWP	Jobcentre Plus	Grants for parents who provide evidence that health advice has been received from a professional and who are in receipt of qualifying benefits. Initial rate was £200, increased to £300 in Autumn 2000, and to £500 in April 2002. Not uprated since April 2002.
Childrens' Fund	2001: announced	Children and Young People's Unit	Local partnerships	Works with children, primarily aged 5 to 13, who are showing early signs of being at risk of social exclusion. Focused on developing services that support multi-agency working, bringing together preventative services that recognise the value of partnership working between the voluntary, community and statutory sectors as well as the beneficiaries of such services. Particular objectives and activities are locally determined. A budget of £450 million for the first three years and £410 million for 2005 to 2008. Now operates in every local authority area in England, with 149 partnerships at local level. Each partnership is overseen by one of nine regional DfES teams. Children's Fund partnerships are required to produce a strategic plan for 2005 to 2008.
Programme for Action	2003: launched	DH	Health partnerships (NHS, local authorities, voluntary and private sectors)	A plan of action to meet the 2004 Public Service Agreement target to reduce health inequalities.
Measures to tackle teenage pregnancy	1999	DH	Schools, clinics, social services, etc	Aims: to halve number of pregnancies in under-18s by 2010, and reduce number by 15% by 2004; and to increase the participation of teenage mothers in education, training or work to 60% by 2010. Budget of £24 million in 2003/2004.
Sure Start Plus	2001: pilot programme 2002: extended to 2006	Sure Start Unit	Local authorities, voluntary sector and Health Action Zones	A pilot programme to provide support for pregnant teenagers and teenage parents and to reduce risk of long-term poverty and social exclusion from teenage pregnancy.

Education

Relevant Public Service Agreement 2004 targets

What	Who
Raise standards in English and maths so that:	
• by 2006, 85% of 11-year-olds achieve Level 4 or above with this level of performance sustained to 2008; and • by 2008, the number of schools in which fewer than 65% of pupils achieve Level 4 or above reduced by 40%.	DfES
Raise standards in English, maths, ICT and science in secondary education so that:	
• by 2007 85% of 14-year-olds achieve Level 5 or above in English, maths and ICT (80% in science) nationally with this level of performance sustained to 2008; and • by 2008, in all schools at least 50% of pupils achieve Level 5 or above in each of English, maths and science.	DfES
By 2008, 60% of those aged 16 to achieve the equivalent of 5 GCSEs at grades A* to C; and in all schools at least 20% of pupils to achieve this standard by 2004, rising to 25% by 2006 and 30% by 2008.	DfES
Increase the proportion of 19-year-olds who achieve at least Level 2 by 3 percentage points between 2004 to 2006, and a further 2 percentage points between 2006 and 2008, and increase the proportion of young people who achieve Level 3.	DfES
Improve levels of school attendance so that by 2008, school absence is reduced by 8% compared to 2003.	DfES

Selected major initiatives under way

Policy	Starting dates	Key department	Key delivery agency	Budget/target/comment
Education Action Zones and Excellence in Cities Action Zones	Successive rounds from 1998 2005: integration of the two programmes	DfES	School-led local partnerships	Aim of Education Action Zones (EAZs) is to raise standards in disadvantaged urban and rural areas, so that young people can become high achievers, effective learners and major contributors to the regeneration of the community. Aim of Excellence in Cities Action Zones (EiC AZs) is to address the educational problems of the major cities where standards have been low. By 2005, all EAZs will become either EiC AZs or 'Excellence Clusters'. By mid-2005, there were 130 EiC AZs. EiC AZs receive up to £350,000 per year.

Policy	Starting dates	Key department	Key delivery agency	Budget/target/comment
National literacy and numeracy strategies	1998: literacy hour and numeracy period introduced 2003: primary strategy launched	DfES	Schools	By 2004, 85% of 11-year-olds to be at Level 4 at key stage 2 in English and Maths. 2,300 summer schools operative by 2000, of which 1,800 were devoted to literacy and numeracy. £240 million over 3 years (+ £16m for summer schools). The Primary Strategy takes the literacy and numeracy strategies under its umbrella.
Tackling truancy and exclusion in schools	1998: new powers to police 1999: LEAs set new targets for schools 2005: Education Regulations	DfES and Home Office	Schools, LEAs and Police	Targets: 1. By 2002, to reduce the number of exclusions by a third from their 1997/98 level. 2. By 2002, to reduce time lost through truancy by a third. 3. By 2008, to reduce school absence by 8% compared to 2003. The National Behaviour and Attendance Strategy aims include: to reduce permanent and fixed term exclusions and to ensure high quality provision for excluded pupils. Budget of £470 million for 2003-2006. By September 2002, schools most affected by unaccounted absenteeism had to produce a strategy with the LEA to reduce absence levels. The 2005 Education (School Attendance Targets) Regulations 2005 require all schools to set absence targets and submit them to their local authority.

In low income households

The number of children in low income households has fallen by 0.7 million since 1996/97 and currently stands at 3.5 million. Children remain more likely than adults to live in low income households.

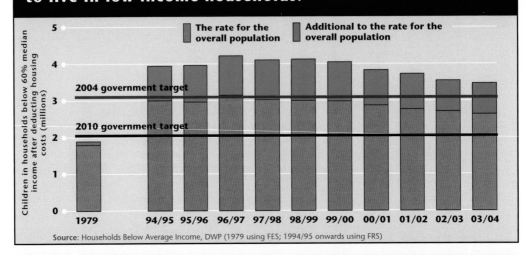

Children in households below 60% median income after deducting housing costs (millions)

The rate for the overall population • Additional to the rate for the overall population

2004 government target

2010 government target

1979 · 94/95 · 95/96 · 96/97 · 97/98 · 98/99 · 99/00 · 00/01 · 01/02 · 02/03 · 03/04

Source: Households Below Average Income, DWP (1979 using FES; 1994/95 onwards using FRS)

Two-fifths of the children in low income households live in couple households where at least one of the adults is in paid work.

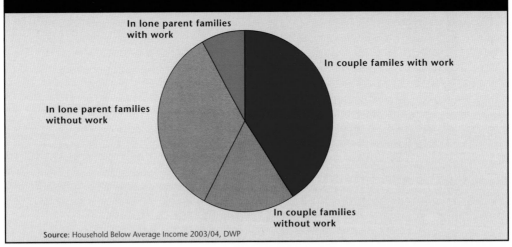

In lone parent families with work

In couple familes with work

In lone parent families without work

In couple families without work

Source: Household Below Average Income 2003/04, DWP

The first graph shows the number of children living in households below 60% of median income after deducting housing costs. The bar is split to show the extent to which children are at a higher risk than adults of being in households below that threshold. The graph also shows the government's targets to reduce the number of children in low income households by a quarter by 2004 and by a half by 2010 compared to the number in 1998/99.

The second graph shows, for the latest year, a breakdown of the children who were in low income households by family type (couple or lone parent) and work status (workless or someone in paid work).

The data source for both graphs is Households Below Average Income, based on the Family Resources Survey (FRS). The data relates to Great Britain. The self-employed are included in the statistics. Income is disposable household income after deducting housing costs. All data is equivalised (adjusted) to account for variation in household size and composition.

Overall adequacy of the indicator: **high**. The FRS is a well-established government survey, designed to be representative of the population as a whole.

In workless households

Indicator
8

The number of children in workless households has fallen by a quarter over the last decade, with most of this fall being for children in couple households.

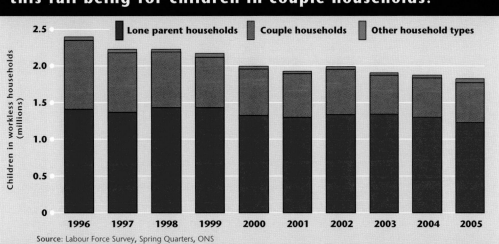

Source: Labour Force Survey, Spring Quarters, ONS

The UK has a higher proportion of its children living in workless households than any other EU country.

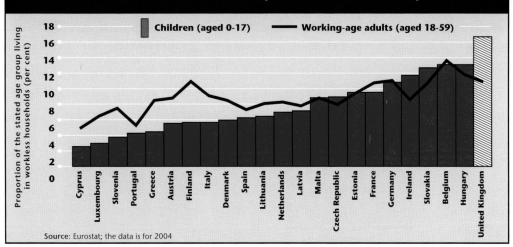

Source: Eurostat; the data is for 2004

The first graph shows the number of children aged under 16 living in households in which none of the working-age adults have paid employment. The data is separated by family type, namely couple households, lone parent households and other households.

The data source is the Labour Force Survey (LFS) and the data for each year is from the Spring Quarter. The data relates to the United Kingdom and is not seasonally adjusted. Working-age households are those with at least one person of working age. Households made up of students and those in which the head of household is retired are excluded.

The second graph shows the proportion of children aged 0–17 in each EU country who live in workless households. For comparison purposes, the equivalent data for 18–59-year-olds is also shown.

The data source is Eurostat, which in turn draws its data from the Labour Force Surveys in each country. The data is for the year 2004.

Overall adequacy of the indicator: **high**. The LFS is a large, well-established, quarterly government survey, designed to be representative of the population as a whole.

Concentrations of poor children

Indicator
9

Half of all the primary school children who are eligible for free school meals are concentrated in a fifth of the schools, a similar proportion to a decade ago.

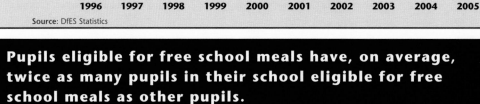

Proportion of children in local education authority primary and nursery schools who are eligible for free school meals who are in the fifth of schools with the highest concentrations of such children (per cent)

Source: DfES Statistics

Pupils eligible for free school meals have, on average, twice as many pupils in their school eligible for free school meals as other pupils.

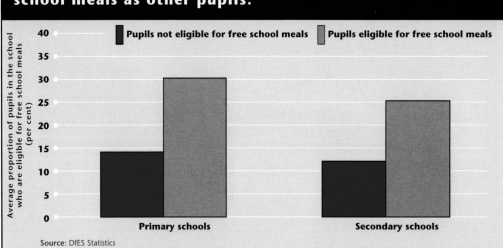

Average proportion of pupils in the school who are eligible for free school meals (per cent)

■ Pupils not eligible for free school meals   ■ Pupils eligible for free school meals

Primary schools   Secondary schools

Source: DfES Statistics

The first graph shows the proportion of children eligible for free school meals who are in the fifth of local education authority primary and nursery schools with the highest concentrations of such children. Note that schools with zero recorded children eligible for free school meals are excluded from the calculations as it is clear that, for some years, some of the zeros represented data gaps rather than true zeros.

For the latest year, the second graph shows that, for children in primary/secondary schools eligible for free school meals, an average of 30%/25% of the children in the school are eligible for free school meals; and for children in primary/secondary schools *not* eligible for free school meals, an average of 14%/12% of the children in the school are eligible for free school meals.

Pupils entitled to free school meals are those within families who receive Income Support (IS) or income-based Jobseeker's Allowance (IBJSA). Those within families who receive support under Part VI of the Immigration and Asylum Act 1999 may also be entitled. Children who receive IS or IBJSA in their own right are also entitled to receive free school meals. Also entitled are children whose parents or carers receive Child Tax Credit, do not receive Working Tax Credit and have an annual income (as assessed by HM Revenue & Customs) of below £13,230 (in 2004).

The data source for both graphs is NPI calculations based on DfES data. The data relates to England.

Overall adequacy of the indicator: **limited**. While the underlying data is sound, its relationship to other aspects of poverty and social exclusion is not immediately clear.

Low birthweight babies

**Indicator
10**

Babies born to parents from manual social backgrounds continue to be more likely to have a low birthweight than those born to parents from non-manual social backgrounds.

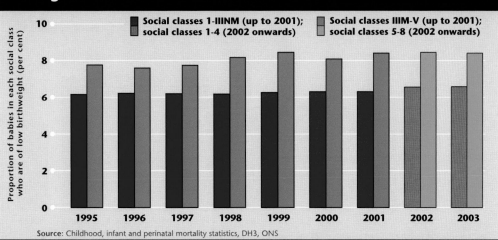

Source: Childhood, infant and perinatal mortality statistics, DH3, ONS

Babies born to lone parents are more likely to be of low birthweight than babies born to couples.

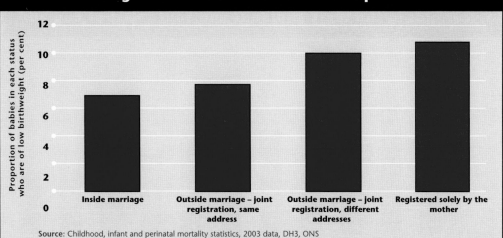

Source: Childhood, infant and perinatal mortality statistics, 2003 data, DH3, ONS

The first graph shows the proportion of babies born each year who are defined as having a low birthweight, ie less than 2^{1}/$_{2}$ kilograms (5^{1}/$_{2}$ lbs). The proportions are shown separately for babies according to the social class of the father. The social class classifications for year 2002 and 2003 are those recently introduced which range from one (higher managerial and professional) to eight (never worked and long-term unemployed). The data is for live-births only (ie it excludes still-births). It is based on a 10% sample coded to father's occupation and excludes sole registrations by mothers.

The second graph shows, for the latest year, how the proportion of babies who are of low birthweight varies according to the parents' marital status at the time of the registration of birth. The data is based on a 100% count of live births.

The data source for both graphs is ONS DH3 statistics and relates to England and Wales.

Overall adequacy of the indicator: **limited**. The data itself is large and reputable, but classification by the social class of the father may be problematic since those where no details are known about the father are not included at all.

Child health and well-being

While the rate of infant deaths among those from non-manual backgrounds has fallen over the last decade, the pattern for those from manual backgrounds is less clear.

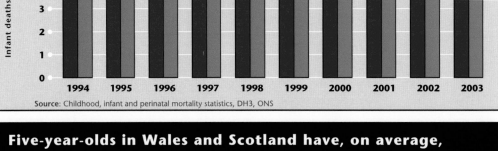

Source: Childhood, infant and perinatal mortality statistics, DH3, ONS

Five-year-olds in Wales and Scotland have, on average, more than twice as many missing, decayed or filled teeth as 5-year-olds in the West Midlands and South East of England.

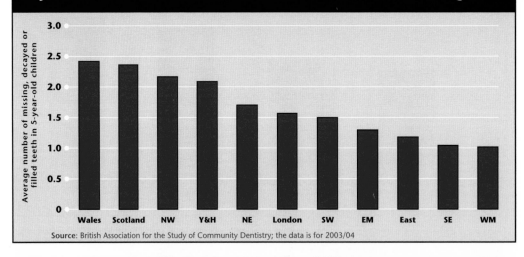

Source: British Association for the Study of Community Dentistry; the data is for 2003/04

The first graph shows the annual number of infant deaths per 1,000 live births, with the data shown separately according to the social class of the father. The social class classifications are those recently introduced which range from one (higher managerial and professional) to eight (never worked and long-term unemployed). Infant deaths are deaths which occur at ages under one year.

The data relates to England and Wales and is based on a 10% sample of live births. The data is based on year of occurrence. Cases where the social class of the father is unknown have been excluded from the analysis.

The second graph shows how the average number of missing, decayed or filled teeth for 5-year-olds varies by region. The data source is a survey of around 190,000 5-year-olds conducted by the British Association for the Study of Community Dentistry. The data relates to Great Britain, with the data for England and Wales being for 2003/04 and the data for Scotland being for 2002/03.

Overall adequacy of the indicator: *high*. The sample sizes are substantial and relatively few have not been coded to a social class.

Underage pregnancies

Indicator
12

While the number of births to girls conceiving under age 16 has fallen by a quarter since 1996, the total number of conceptions has remained unchanged because of an increased number of abortions.

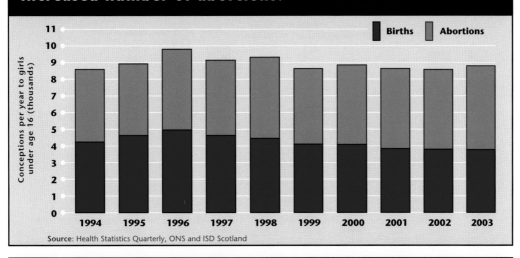

Source: Health Statistics Quarterly, ONS and ISD Scotland

Teenage motherhood is seven times as common amongst those from manual social backgrounds as for those from professional backgrounds.

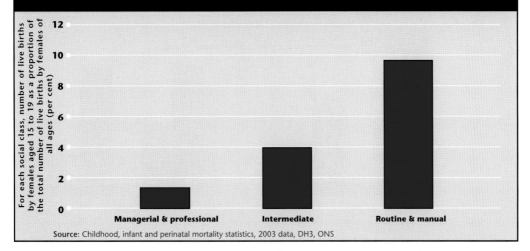

Source: Childhood, infant and perinatal mortality statistics, 2003 data, DH3, ONS

The first graph shows the number of conceptions per year to girls conceiving under the age of 16, with the data shown separately for delivered babies and for abortions.

The data relates to Great Britain. English and Welsh conceptions leading to births are counted during the actual year of conception, whilst Scottish conceptions are counted after the birth of the child, which is commonly in the calendar year following conception. ONS population projections have been used for the number of 15-year-old girls.

The second graph shows, for the latest year, the number of live births by females aged 15 to 19 in each social class as a proportion of the total live births by females of that social class. The data source is the DH3 mortality statistics from ONS. The analysis is based on the recorded social class of the father of the baby. As such, it does not include the 25% of births to females aged 15 to 19 which were sole registrations.

Overall adequacy of the indicator: **medium**. The collection of the conception and births statistics is an established process.

Low attainment at school (11-year-olds)

Progress continues to be made in the literacy and numeracy of 11-year-olds – including those in deprived schools – but the rate of progress has slowed in recent years.

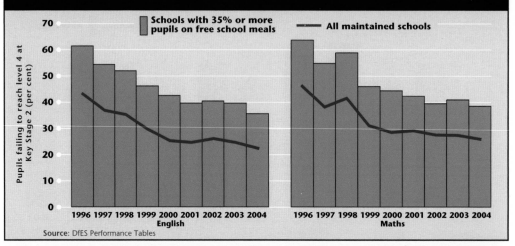

Source: DfES Performance Tables

11-year-old pupils in receipt of free school meals are twice as likely not to achieve basic standards in literacy and numeracy as other 11-year-old pupils.

Source: National Curriculum Assessment GCSE and Equivalent Attainment and Post-16 Attainment by Pupil Characteristics in England, DfES, 2005; the data is for 2004

The first graph compares the proportion of children failing to reach Level 4 at Key Stage 2 (11 years old) in schools which have at least 35% of pupils receiving free school meals with that for all maintained mainstream schools. The graph shows maths and English separately and shows changes over time. The data source is DfES performance tables. The data relates to England and covers all LEA maintained schools.

The second graph shows how the proportion of children failing to achieve Level 4 at Key Stage 2 varies by gender and whether or not the pupil is in receipt of free school meals. The data source is a DfES publication entitled National Curriculum Assessment GCSE and Equivalent Attainment and Post-16 Attainment by Pupil Characteristics in England, published in February 2005. The data relates to England, covers all maintained schools and is for 2004.

Overall adequacy of the indicator: ***medium***. While the data itself is sound enough, the choice of the particular level of exam success is a matter of judgement.

Low attainment at school
(16-year-olds)

Twelve per cent of 16-year-olds still obtain fewer than 5 GCSEs and 6 per cent get no GCSEs at all, both figures being unchanged since 1998/99.

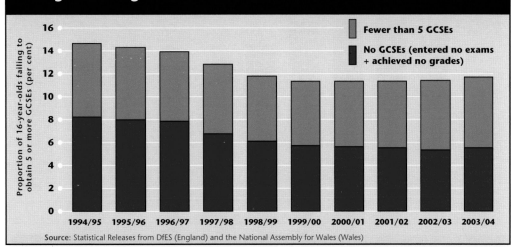

Source: Statistical Releases from DfES (England) and the National Assembly for Wales (Wales)

Three-quarters of pupils in receipt of free school meals do not obtain 5 or more GCSEs at grade C or above. This compares with less than half of other pupils.

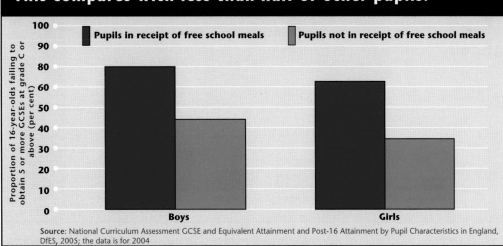

Source: National Curriculum Assessment GCSE and Equivalent Attainment and Post-16 Attainment by Pupil Characteristics in England, DfES, 2005; the data is for 2004

The first graph shows the proportion of students (defined as pupils aged 15 at 31 August in the calendar year prior to sitting the exams) failing to obtain five or more GCSEs in England and Wales. The numbers are split between those who obtain no GCSE grade at all, either because they don't enter for exams or achieve no passes, and those who do obtain some GCSEs but less than five. The data sources are DfES and the Welsh Assembly. The data relates to England and Wales and covers all schools including city technology colleges and academies, community and foundation special schools, hospital schools, pupil referral units and non-maintained special schools.

The second graph shows how the proportion of children failing to achieve five or more GCSEs at grade C or above varies by gender and whether or not the pupil is in receipt of free school meals (such data is only available for this threshold, which is much higher than the threshold used in the other graphs). The data source is a DfES publication entitled *National Curriculum Assessment GCSE and Equivalent Attainment and Post-16 Attainment by Pupil Characteristics in England*, published in February 2005. The data relates to England, covers all maintained schools and is for 2004.

Overall adequacy of the indicator: **medium**. While the data itself is sound enough, the choice of the particular level of exam success is a matter of judgement.

School exclusions

**Indicator
15**

The number of permanent exclusions has been increasing since 1999.

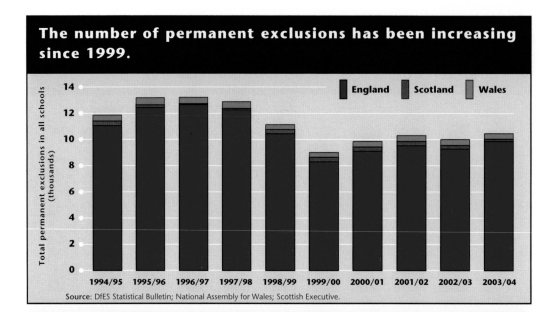

Source: DfES Statistical Bulletin; National Assembly for Wales; Scottish Executive.

The rate of permanent exclusions of Black Caribbean pupils has halved in recent years, but they are still three times as likely to be excluded as white pupils.

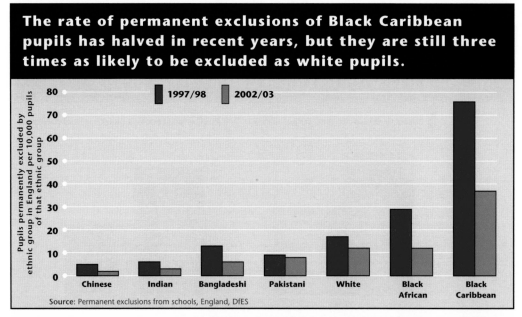

Source: Permanent exclusions from schools, England, DfES

The first graph shows the number of pupils permanently excluded from primary, secondary and special schools. The data relates to Great Britain. In Scotland, the data (referred to as 'removals from register') was collected from local authorities via a new survey from 1998/99. Previously, this information had been collected from individual schools. Data from 1994/95 to 1997/98 for Scotland is therefore not strictly comparable with the more recent figures.

The second graph shows the rate of exclusion for children from different ethnic backgrounds in 1997/98 and 2002/03 (the latest year for which data is available). The data relates to England only.

Overall adequacy of the indicator: **medium**. Exclusions are susceptible to administrative procedures; for example, these officially recorded numbers may well under-represent the true number of exclusions if parents are persuaded to withdraw their child rather than leave the school to exclude them.

3 Young adults

This chapter has two themes containing six indicators. The themes are:

- transitions to adulthood;
- economic circumstances.

Transitions to adulthood
Choice of indicators
The three indicators here cover quite different aspects of transition from childhood to adulthood and from education to work. The first indicator shows the number of 19-year-olds without either any qualification or very limited ones only. The supporting graph shows how the proportion with various levels of qualification varies by age, from the age of 16 to the age of 25.

The second indicator looks at 16-year-olds who are in neither education nor training and how this percentage has changed since the mid-1990s. The second graph looks at entry rates to university according to the level of deprivation in the student's home area.

The third graph shows the number of 18- to 20-year-olds found guilty of an indictable offence and how that number has changed over the last decade. The supporting graph shows the proportion of 16- to 20-year-olds in prison for different ethnic groups.

What the indicators show
Indicator 16 Without a basic qualification
One in four 19-year-olds still fail to achieve a basic level of qualification. One in thirteen have no qualifications at all.

Most 17-year-olds with five or more good GCSEs go on to achieve further qualifications, but most 17-year-olds without such qualifications still lack NVQ2 or equivalent at age 25.

Indicator 17 School leavers
One in six of all 16-year-olds are not in education or training. This proportion has not fallen since 2000.

In the most deprived wards, it was rare at the end of the 1990s for more than a quarter of 18-year-olds to go to higher education. In the least deprived wards, it was normal.

Indicator 18 With a criminal record
The number of 18- to 20-year-olds found guilty of an indictable offence has been falling steadily over the last few years and is now a fifth lower than in 1999.

Black young adults are four times as likely as white young adults to be in prison.

Economic circumstances
Choice of indicators

The first indicator for this theme shows the proportion of those aged 16 to 24 who are living in low income households over time compared with the rate for adults aged 25 to retirement. The supporting graph shows these rates according to the economic status of the household in which the young adult is living.

The other two indicators show the proportion of young adults under 25 who are unemployed and the proportion of those aged under 22 who are low paid. In both cases, the supporting graphs, which show the rates of both unemployment and low pay among those aged 25 to 29 according to the level of qualifications, are as important as the main graphs. This is because they show the connection between educational outcomes in late teens and future economic prospects.

What the indicators show
Indicator 19 In low income households

Young adults are much more likely to live in low income households than older working-age adults.

Unemployed young adults are less likely to be in a low income household than their older counterparts.

Indicator 20 Unemployment

The unemployment rate for 18- to 24-year-olds has fallen by a quarter over the last decade. But it is now three times the rate for older workers, which has halved over the same period.

The lower a young adult's qualifications, the more likely they are to be unemployed. But, except for those with no qualifications, the vast majority are still employed.

Indicator 21 Low pay

Almost three-quarters of employees aged 18 to 21 – both male and female – earned less than £6.50 per hour in 2004 (equivalent to £5.00 per hour in 1998 after uprating for the average rise in earnings).

The lower a young adult's qualifications, the more likely they are to be low paid.

Relevant Public Service Agreement 2004 targets

What	Who
Increase the proportion of 19-year-olds who achieve at least Level 2 by 3 percentage points between 2004 to 2006, and a further 2 percentage points between 2006 and 2008, and increase the proportion of young people who achieve Level 3.	DfES
Reduce the proportion of young people not in education, employment or training by 2 percentage points by 2010.	DfES
As part of the wider objective of full employment in every region, over the three years to Spring 2008, and taking account of the economic cycle: • increase the employment rates of disadvantaged groups (lone parents, ethnic minorities, people aged 50 and over, those with the lowest qualifications, and those living in local authority wards with the poorest initial labour market position); and • significantly reduce the difference between the employment rates of the disadvantaged groups and the overall rate.	DWP
As part of the wider objective of full employment in every region, over the three years to Spring 2008, and taking account of the economic cycle, demonstrate progress on increasing the employment rate.	DWP and HM Treasury

Selected major initiatives under way (Also see the Low Income chapter.)

Policy	Starting dates	Key department	Key delivery agency	Budget/target/comment
Improving participation and attainment of 14- to 19-year-olds	1997: introduced 2000: widened 2004: updated	DfES	Careers service and schools	Targets (14-year-olds): • By 2007, 85% to achieve Level 5 or above in each of the key stage 3 tests in English, maths and ICT, and 80% in science. Targets (16-year-olds): • Increase the percentage of pupils obtaining 5 or more GCSEs at grade A*-C by 2 percentage points each year between 2002 and 2006. By 2004, all Local Education Authorities to have a rate of at least 38% of 16-year-old pupils obtaining five or more GCSEs at grade A*-C or equivalent. • Increase the percentage of pupils obtaining 5 or more GCSEs at grade A*-G (including English and maths by 2004). By 2004, 92% of 16-year-olds should reach this standard. Targets (19-year-olds): • By 2004, increase by 3 percentage points the number of 19-year-olds achieving a qualification equivalent to NVQ Level 2 compared to 2002. Updated in 2004 as part of the Five Year Strategy for Children and Learners.
Education Maintenance Allowance	1999: introduced 2004: to be rolled out nationally	DfES	LEAs, schools, colleges, and the Careers Service	The scheme is being rolled out nationally from September 2004, and will include a £30 weekly payment and periodic bonuses if the student keeps to the terms of their 'learning agreement'.

Policy	Starting dates	Key department	Key delivery agency	Budget/target/comment
Connexions (replacing Careers Service)	2000: pilots 2001: phased launch 2003: extended to cover all of England.	National Unit for Connexions Service	Local Connexions partnerships	A universal service providing advice, guidance and support for 13- to 19-year-olds, in particular to connect and reconnect with learning. Brings together new and existing services to a coherent whole. A key objective is to increase post-16 participation and to reduce the number of young people not in education, employment or training. Various targets involving education, care, drugs, offending and teenage pregnancy. A budget of £320 million in 2001/02, covering both Connexions (£110 million) and the Careers Service (£210 million). A budget of £420 million for 2002/03, £460 million for 2003/04 and £455 million for 2004/05.
New Deal for 18- to 24-year-olds	1998: introduced 2001: made permanent 2002: Jobcentre Plus rollout nationwide	DfES/DWP	Jobcentre Plus with variety of local partnerships	Aims to move young adults into work. Government figures are that 560,000 young people moved into jobs by March 2005, 80% of which were sustained jobs and 20% lasted less than 13 weeks. Budget of £2.6 billion from 1998 to 2004.

Without a basic qualification

Indicator
16

One in four 19-year-olds still fail to achieve a basic level of qualification. One in thirteen have no qualifications at all.

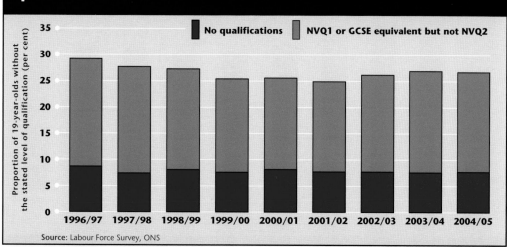

Source: Labour Force Survey, ONS

Most 17-year-olds with 5 or more good GCSEs go on to achieve further qualifications, but most 17-year-olds without such qualifications still lack NVQ2 or equivalent at age 25.

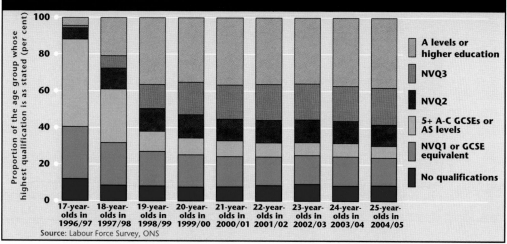

Source: Labour Force Survey, ONS

The first graph shows the proportion of 19-year-olds without a basic qualification, with the data shown separately for those without NVQ2 or equivalent and those without any GCSEs at grade G or above. To improve statistical reliability, the figures for each year are the averages for the four quarters to the relevant Winter quarter.

DfES equivalence scales have been used to translate academic qualifications into their vocational equivalents. So, for example, 'NVQ2 or equivalent' includes those with five GCSEs at grade C or above, GNVQ level 2, two AS levels or one A level. In line with these equivalence scales, 35% of those with an 'other qualification' are considered to have NVQ2 or equivalent and a further 10% are considered to have NVQ3 or equivalent.

The second graph shows how the proportion of young adults with various levels of highest qualification varies by age. The levels of qualification shown are a mixture of academic and vocational qualifications, namely A level or higher education, NVQ3, NVQ2, 5+ A–C GCSEs or AS levels, NVQ1 or GCSE equivalent, and no qualifications. The ages shown are 17 to 25. To show how young adults gain higher qualifications as they grow older, the data is for the same group of individuals namely those who were 25 in 2004/05, 24 in 2003/04, 23 in 2002/03 etc.

The data source for both graphs is the Labour Force Survey (LFS) and relates to the United Kingdom. Respondents who did not answer the questions required to perform the analysis have been excluded from the relevant graphs.

Overall adequacy of the indicator: **high**. The LFS is a well-established, quarterly survey designed to be representative of the population as whole.

School leavers

Indicator
17

One in six of all 16-year-olds are not in education or training. This proportion has not fallen since 2000.

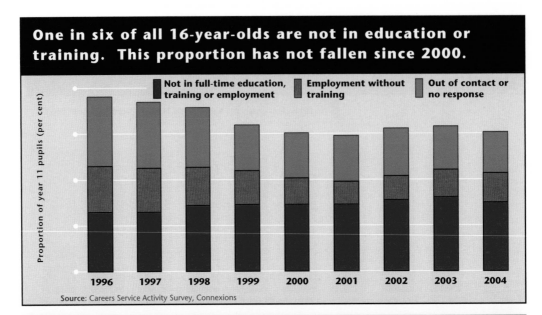

Source: Careers Service Activity Survey, Connexions

In the most deprived wards, it was rare at the end of the 1990s for more than a quarter of 18-year-olds to go to higher education. In the least deprived wards, it was normal.

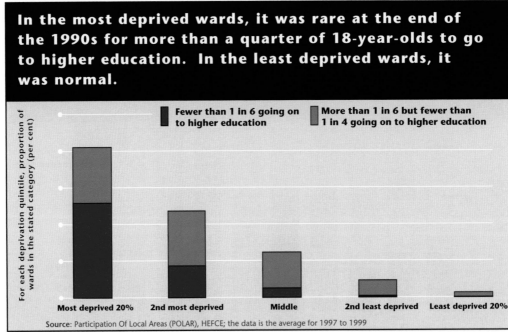

Source: Participation Of Local Areas (POLAR), HEFCE; the data is the average for 1997 to 1999

The first graph shows the proportion of year 11 pupils who are not in full-time education or training. The data source is the Connexions Careers Service Activity Survey. The data relates to England only. 'Out of contact or no response' effectively means that Connexions has lost contact with the person.

The second graph shows how the proportion of young adults who go on to higher education varies by electoral ward. The wards are grouped by level of deprivation and, for each group, the graph shows the proportion of the wards in this group where fewer than 16% and between 16% and 24% of the young adults go on higher education. The data source is participation of local areas (POLAR) data published by the Higher Education Funding Council for England (HEFCE). The data is for England only and is the average for the years 1997 to 1999 (the latest data available). The data used to divide the wards in deprivation groupings is the 2000 Index of Multiple Deprivation.

Overall adequacy of the indicator: **high**. The Careers Service Activity Survey is a well-established government survey.

With a criminal record

Indicator
18

The number of 18- to 20-year-olds found guilty of an indictable offence has been falling steadily over the last few years and is now a fifth lower than in 1999.

Women
Men

18- to 20-year-olds found guilty of an indictable offence (thousands)

| 1994 | 1995 | 1996 | 1997 | 1998 | 1999 | 2000 | 2001 | 2002 | 2003 |

Source: Criminal Statistics England and Wales, Home Office

Black young adults are four times as likely as white young adults to be in prison.

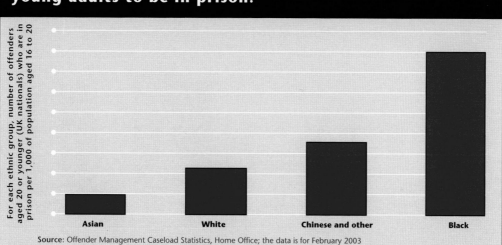

For each ethnic group, number of offenders aged 20 or younger (UK nationals) who are in prison per 1,000 of population aged 16 to 20

Asian   White   Chinese and other   Black

Source: Offender Management Caseload Statistics, Home Office; the data is for February 2003

The first graph shows the number of young men and women aged 18 to 20 who were convicted of an indictable offence in each year. The data source is the Home Office's Criminal Statistics for England and Wales.

The second graph shows, for the latest year, the likelihood of being in prison under sentence across different ethnic groups. These likelihoods are expressed in terms of the number of offenders aged 20 or younger sentenced who are UK nationals and in prison in June 2002 per 1,000 population aged 16 to 20 of the relevant ethnic group. The data source is the Home Office Prison Statistics for England and Wales. 'Asians' include people from Bangladeshi, Indian and Pakistani communities. 'Chinese and other' includes people from other Asian communities, Chinese ethnic groups and other. The figures are for UK nationals only and therefore exclude foreign nationals, with it being assumed that the prison proportion who are foreign nationals is similar for the 16 to 20 age group as for the all-age proportions.

Overall adequacy of the indicator: **medium**. The data is dependent upon administrative practices of the police and the judicial system.

In low income households

Indicator 19

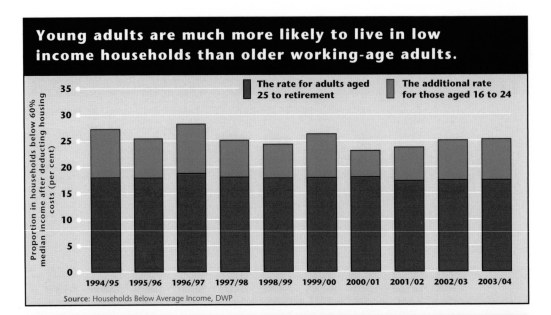

Young adults are much more likely to live in low income households than older working-age adults.

Legend: The rate for adults aged 25 to retirement | The additional rate for those aged 16 to 24

Y-axis: Proportion in households below 60% median income after deducting housing costs (per cent)

Years: 1994/95, 1995/96, 1996/97, 1997/98, 1998/99, 1999/00, 2000/01, 2001/02, 2002/03, 2003/04

Source: Households Below Average Income, DWP

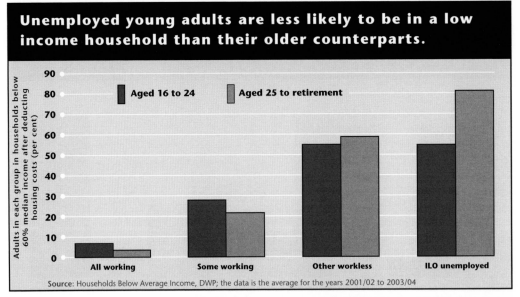

Unemployed young adults are less likely to be in a low income household than their older counterparts.

Legend: Aged 16 to 24 | Aged 25 to retirement

Y-axis: Adults in each group in households below 60% median income after deducting housing costs (per cent)

Categories: All working, Some working, Other workless, ILO unemployed

Source: Households Below Average Income, DWP; the data is the average for the years 2001/02 to 2003/04

The first graph shows the proportion of adults aged 16 to 24 living in households below 60% of median income after deducting housing costs. The bar is split to show the extent to which adults aged 16 to 24 are at a higher risk than older working-age adults of being in households below that threshold.

The second graph shows how the risks of being in low income vary by work status, with the data shown separately for adults aged 16 to 24 and from 25 to retirement. The following work statuses are shown: all working (single or couple, with one in full-time work and the other – if applicable – in full-time or part-time work); some working (includes households where no one is working full-time but one or more are working part-time); unemployed (head or spouse unemployed) and other workless (includes students and lone parents). To improve statistical reliability, the data is averaged for the years 2001/02 to 2003/04.

The data source for both graphs is Households Below Average Income, based on the Family Resources Survey (FRS). The data relates to Great Britain. The self-employed are included in the first graph but not the second. Income is disposable household income after deducting housing costs. All data is equivalised (adjusted) to account for variation in household size and composition.

Overall adequacy of the indicator: **high**. The FRS is a well-established government survey, designed to be representative of the population as a whole.

Unemployment

The unemployment rate for 18- to 24-year-olds has fallen by a quarter over the last decade. But it is now three times the rate for older workers, which has halved over the same period.

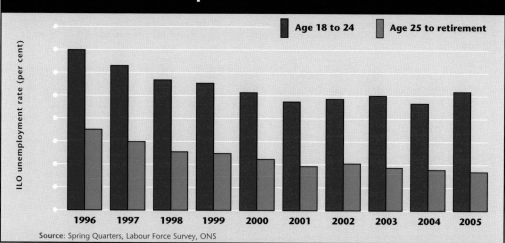

Source: Spring Quarters, Labour Force Survey, ONS

The lower a young adult's qualifications, the more likely they are to be unemployed. But, except for those with no qualifications, the vast majority are still employed.

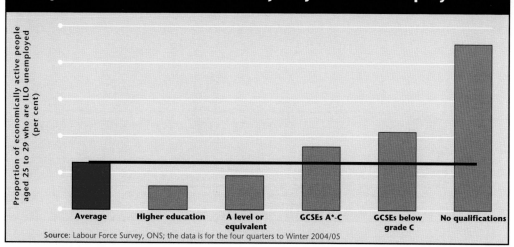

Source: Labour Force Survey, ONS; the data is for the four quarters to Winter 2004/05

The first graph shows the proportion of those aged 18 to 24 who are unemployed compared with those aged 25 and over (up to retirement). The data source is the Labour Force Survey (LFS) and the data for each year is from the Spring Quarter. The data relates to the United Kingdom and is not seasonally adjusted. 'Unemployment' is the ILO definition, which is used for the official UK unemployment numbers. It includes all those with no paid work in the survey week who were available to start work in the next fortnight and who either looked for work in the last month or were waiting to start a job already obtained. The ILO unemployment rate is the percentage of the economically active population who are unemployed on the ILO measure (ie the total population for the relevant age group less those classified as economically inactive). So, for example, it excludes those still in education.

The second graph shows the proportion of economically active 25- to 29-year-olds who are ILO unemployed, with the data broken down by level of highest qualification. The lower age limit of 25 has been chosen on the grounds that a) the vast majority of people will have completed their formal education by that age and b) they will no longer be in casual employment (as, for example, students often are). To improve statistical reliability, the data is averaged for the four quarters to Winter 2004/05. The data source is the Labour Force Survey (LFS) and relates to the United Kingdom. Respondents who did not answer the questions required to perform the analysis have been excluded from the relevant graphs.

Overall adequacy of the indicator: **high**. The LFS is a large, well-established, quarterly government survey, designed to be representative of the population as a whole.

Low pay

Almost three-quarters of employees aged 18 to 21 – both male and female – earned less than £6.50 per hour in 2004 (equivalent to £5.00 per hour in 1998 after uprating for the average rise in earnings).

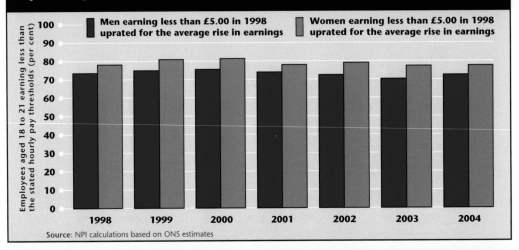

Legend: **Men earning less than £5.00 in 1998 uprated for the average rise in earnings** | **Women earning less than £5.00 in 1998 uprated for the average rise in earnings**

Y-axis: Employees aged 18 to 21 earning less than the stated hourly pay thresholds (per cent)

X-axis: 1998, 1999, 2000, 2001, 2002, 2003, 2004

Source: NPI calculations based on ONS estimates

The lower a young adult's qualifications, the more likely they are to be low paid.

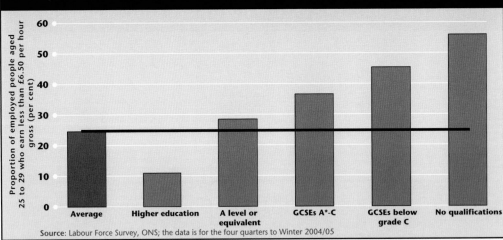

Y-axis: Proportion of employed people aged 25 to 29 who earn less than £6.50 per hour gross (per cent)

X-axis: Average, Higher education, A level or equivalent, GCSEs A*-C, GCSEs below grade C, No qualifications

Source: Labour Force Survey, ONS; the data is for the four quarters to Winter 2004/05

The first graph shows the estimated proportion of employees aged 18 to 21 who were paid below various hourly rates of pay in each year shown. No data is available for years before 1998 and the available data only distinguishes between the 18 to 21 and 22+ age groups. The low paid threshold used aims to reflect average rise in earnings and rises in line with the ONS Average Earnings Index from a base of £5.00 per hour in 1998. It is therefore £5.22 in 1999, £5.51 in 2000, £5.78 in 2001, £5.95 in 2002, £6.14 in 2003 and £6.46 in 2004. The figures are from published ONS statistics which were themselves derived from a combination of data from the Labour Force Survey (LFS) and Annual Survey of Hours and Earnings (ASHE), with adjustments by the ONS.

The second graph shows the proportion of 25- to 29-year-olds who are in employment who have an average hourly gross pay of less than £6.50, with the data broken down by level of highest qualification. The lower age limit of 25 has been chosen on the grounds that a) the vast majority of people will have completed their formal education by that age and b) they will no longer be in casual employment (as, for example, students often are). To improve statistical reliability, the data is averaged for the four quarters to Winter 2004/05. The data source is the Labour Force Survey (LFS) and relates to the United Kingdom. Respondents who did not answer the questions required to perform the analysis have been excluded from the relevant graphs.

Overall adequacy of the indicator: ***medium***. The LFS and ASHE are well-established government surveys, designed to be representative of the population as a whole. However, the ONS methods for combining and adjusting the data are not available for public scrutiny, and the underlying dataset itself is not publicly available. In other words, outside researchers have to rely on whatever data ONS decides to publish.

4 Working-age adults aged 25+

This chapter has five themes containing 13 indicators. A strand running through most of the themes, reflecting a particular interest of this report, is the difference that disability makes to many of the things measured here. The five themes are:

- economic circumstances;
- exclusion from work;
- low pay;
- disadvantaged at work;
- health and well-being.

Economic circumstances

Choice of indicators

The first indicator focuses on how the percentage of people aged 25 to retirement who are in low income households has changed, comparing the three most recent years with three years in the mid-1990s. The first graph shows the percentages by household work status while the supporting graph shows the share which each work status category takes of the total number of working-age adults in low income.

The second indicator contrasts the situation of disabled and non-disabled adults as far as income poverty is concerned. The first graph shows the percentage of each group in low income households. The supporting graph shows how this percentage varies between disabled and non-disabled people according to the work status of the household they live in.

What the indicators show

Indicator 22 Low income and work

A household's risk of low income varies greatly depending on how much paid work it does. These risks have increased somewhat for all household types since the mid-1990s.

Among those aged 25 to retirement in low income households, the proportion where the head of the household is unemployed has halved. Almost half now have someone in paid work.

Indicator 23 Low income and disability

Disabled adults are twice as likely to live in low income households as non-disabled adults, and the gap has grown over the last decade.

Disabled people in workless households are somewhat less likely to be in low income than their non-disabled counterparts.

Exclusion from work

Choice of indicators

The first indicator focuses on the number of people aged 25 to retirement who are either unemployed or economically inactive but wanting work (which together make up those described as 'lacking but wanting work'). The first graph shows the percentages for each group for each of the last ten years. The supporting graph breaks down all those 'lacking but wanting work' into the number who are unemployed and the numbers who are economically inactive by the reason for it.

The first graph of the second indicator is a development of the first graph of the previous one, showing this time for disabled and non-disabled people separately the percentages either unemployed or economically inactive but wanting work. These percentages are shown for each year back to the late 1990s. The supporting graph shows the percentage 'lacking but wanting work', separately for disabled and non-disabled people, according to their highest level of qualification. These qualifications range from a higher education degree through to no qualification at all.

The third indicator focuses on workless households. The first graph shows the percentages of all working-age households who are workless according to whether they are single adult households or not and also according to whether the households have children living in them. These percentages are shown for each of the last ten years. The supporting graph breaks down both the number of adults and the number of children in workless, working-age households according to whether they are single adult households or not.

What the indicators show
Indicator 24 Wanting paid work
Whereas the number officially unemployed has halved over the last decade, the number who are 'economically inactive but want work' has only fallen by a seventh.

A third of those wanting paid work are unemployed. A further quarter are long-term sick or disabled.

Indicator 25 Work and disability
One in five adults with a work-limiting disability is not working but wants to. This compares with one in fifteen of those with no work-limiting disability.

At all levels of qualification, the proportion of people with a work-limiting disability who lack but want paid work is much greater than for those without a work-limiting disability.

Indicator 26 Workless households
While the number of 2+ adult working-age households who are workless has fallen, the number of single adult households who are workless has not.

Three-fifths of people in workless working-age households are living in single adult households.

Low pay
Choice of indicators
Throughout this theme and elsewhere, low pay is defined as £6.50 an hour or less in 2004, which was equivalent to £5 an hour in 1998 after uprating for the rise in average earnings. In all cases, the statistics are for those aged 25 to retirement.

The first indicator shows the principal statistics on the extent of low pay among people aged 25 to retirement, separately for men and women. The first graph shows the numbers of low paid men and women for each year since 1998. The supporting graph breaks the number for the latest year down further between both men and women and full-and part-time employment.

The second indicator looks at low pay by industry sectors such as retail, the public sector and manufacturing. The first graph shows the percentages of all workers in the industry or sector who are low paid, men and women shown separately. The supporting graph shows what share of the total number of low paid employees each industry/sector takes.

The third indicator compares the likelihood of low pay according to whether a person is disabled or not. The first graph shows the percentage of low paid employees, separately for male and female full-time workers as well as part-time workers, dividing each between those who are disabled and those who are not. The supporting graph shows the percentage of employees who are low paid, separately for disabled and non-disabled people, according to their highest level of qualification, ranging from a higher education degree through to no qualification at all.

What the indicators show
Indicator 27 Low pay by gender
3.7 million female employees aged 22 and over – and 1.8 million male employees – were paid less than £6.50 per hour in 2004 (equivalent to £5.00 per hour in 1998 after uprating for the average rise in earnings).

Around half of those paid less than £6.50 per hour are part-time workers, mainly women.

Indicator 28 Low pay by industry
Around half of employees aged 25 and over in the hotels and restaurants and wholesale and retail sectors earn less than £6.50 per hour. In both sectors, two-thirds of these are women.

Almost a third of all employees aged 25 to retirement earning less than £6.50 per hour work in the public sector.

Indicator 29 Low pay and disability
For both full-time and part-time work, the proportion of employees with a work-limiting disability who are low paid is around 10 per cent higher than that for employees without a work-limiting disability.

At all levels of qualification, the risk of someone with a work-limiting disability being low paid is somewhat higher than that for someone without a work-limiting disability.

Disadvantaged at work
Choice of indicators
The two indicators for this theme address four different aspects of disadvantage at work. The first indicator addresses jobs that are in some respect unsatisfactory. The first graph shows the number of people making a new claim for Jobseeker's Allowance – the benefit for people who are unemployed – within six months of last claiming. It is therefore, in effect, a measure of the extent to which the unemployed take jobs that turn out to be short-term ones only. The supporting graph develops this idea by showing, separately for people in part-time jobs and people in temporary employment, the extent to which people are in these jobs because they cannot find other ones.

The first graph of the second indicator shows the percentage of people aged 25 to retirement in work who have recently received work-related training in each of the last 10 years, the percentages being shown separately for people with and without qualifications. The supporting graph, on a quite different subject, shows the proportion of employees belonging to a trade union according to their hourly rate of pay.

What the indicators show
Indicator 30 Insecure at work
Almost half of the men, and a third of the women, making a new claim for Jobseeker's Allowance were last claiming less than six months ago. These proportions are similar to a decade ago.

Only one in twelve part-time employees want a full-time job – but more than a quarter of temporary employees would like a permanent job.

Indicator 31 Support at work
Although there has been some improvement over the last decade, people with no qualifications are still three times less likely to receive job-related training than those with some qualifications.

Fifteen per cent of workers earning less than £6.50 an hour belong to a trade union compared with 40 per cent of those earning £9 to £21 an hour.

Health and well-being
Choice of indicators
The first indicator here shows the proportion of both men and women aged under 65 who have died in each of the last ten years. The supporting graph, again for men and women separately, shows the rates of deaths for the principal causes, namely heart disease and lung cancer, by social class.

The second indicator relates to the percentage of people aged 45 to 64 who report a longstanding illness or disability which limits their activity. The first graph shows these percentages annually over the last decade, separately for men and women. The supporting graph reports the latest year's figures, again for men and women separately, according to the person's level of income.

The final indicator is of similar kind, but this time the subject is people who are judged to be at high risk of developing a mental illness. Again, the first graph shows the percentages for both men and women, annually over the last decade. The supporting graph reports the latest year's figures, again for men and women separately, according to the person's level of income.

What the indicators show
Indicator 32 Premature death
The rate of premature death fell by one-tenth in the decade to 2003. It is, however, still one-and-a-half times as high among men as among women.

Death rates from heart disease and lung cancer – the two biggest causes of premature death – for people aged 35 to 64 are around twice as high among those from manual backgrounds as from non-manual backgrounds.

Indicator 33 Limiting longstanding illness
A quarter of adults aged 45–64 suffer a longstanding illness or disability which limits their activity.

Almost half of all adults in the poorest fifth of the population aged 45–64 have a limiting longstanding illness or disability, twice the rate for those on average incomes.

Indicator 34 Mental health
The proportion of adults aged 25 to retirement who are at a high risk of developing a mental illness is similar to a decade ago. Women are more at risk than men.

Adults in the poorest fifth are twice as likely to be at risk of developing a mental illness as those on average incomes.

Economic circumstances
Relevant Public Service Agreement 2004 targets

What	Who
Halve the number of children in relative low income households between 1998/99 and 2010/11, on the way to eradicating child poverty by 2020, including:	DWP and HMT
• reducing the proportion of children in workless households by 5% between spring 2005 and spring 2008; and • increasing the proportion of parents with care on Income Support and income-based Jobseeker's Allowance who receive maintenance for their children by 65% by March 2008.	

Selected major initiatives under way
See the Low Income chapter.

Exclusion from work
Relevant Public Service Agreement 2004 targets

What	Who
As a contribution to reducing the proportion of children living in households where no-one is working by 2008:	DWP
• increase the stock of Ofsted-registered childcare by 10%; • increase the take-up of formal childcare by lower income working families by 50%; and • introduce a successful light-touch childcare approval scheme by April 2005.	
As part of the wider objective of full employment in every region, over the three years to spring 2008, and taking account of the economic cycle:	DWP
• increase the employment rates of disadvantaged groups (lone parents, ethnic minorities, people aged 50 and over, those with the lowest qualifications, and those living in local authority wards with the poorest initial labour market position); and • significantly reduce the difference between the employment rates of the disadvantaged groups and the overall rate.	
As part of the wider objective of full employment in every region, over the three years to spring 2008, and taking account of the economic cycle, demonstrate progress on increasing the employment rate.	DWP and HM Treasury
By 2008, working with all departments, bring about measurable improvements in gender equality across a range of indicators, as part of the Government's objectives on equality and social inclusion.	DTI

Selected major initiatives under way

Policy	Starting dates	Key department	Key delivery agency	Budget/target/comment
New Deal for disabled people	1998: introduced 2001: extended	DfES/DWP	Jobcentre Plus with variety of local partnerships	Government figures are that 75,000 disabled people moved into jobs by March 2005. A budget of £20 million each year from 2000/01 to 2004.
New Deal for lone parents	1997: prototype 1998: national rollout 2000: uprated and extended	DfES/DWP	Jobcentre Plus with variety of local partnerships	Aims to achieve an overall 70% employment for lone parents by 2010. Government figures are that 380,000 lone parents moved into jobs by March 2005. Around half of the leavers from the scheme leave for employment and a third leave for other reasons but remain on Income Support. A budget of £100 million for 2001/02, £180 million for 2002/03 and £250 million for 2003/04. In the 2003 Budget, it was announced that a national mentoring service would be introduced.
New Deal for the over 50s	November 1999: pathfinders April 2000: implementation	DfES/DWP	Jobcentre Plus with variety of local partnerships	Government figures are that 40,000 people moved into jobs between April 2003 and March 2005. A voluntary scheme and, overall, 1 million people are eligible to participate. Includes payments of tax-free employment credit, a training grant, and support and advice. A budget of £20 million for each year from 2000/01 until 2004.
New Deal for partners of unemployed people	1999: started 2000: became mandatory	DfES/DWP	Jobcentre Plus with variety of local partnerships	Aimed to move 3,000 eligible people into work in 2000/01 and a further 3,000 in 2001/02. A budget of £20 million for each year from 2000/01 until 2004. From April 2004, partners are entitled to the same help and support as lone parents.

Low Pay

Relevant Public Service Agreement 2004 targets

None identified.

Selected major initiatives under way

See the Low Income chapter.

Disadvantaged at work
Relevant Public Service Agreement 2004 targets

What	Who
Increase the number of adults with the skills required for employability and progression to higher levels of training through:	DfES
• improving the basic skill levels of 2.25 million adults between the launch of Skills for Life in 2001 and 2010, with a milestone of 1.5 million in 2007; and • reducing by at least 40% the number of adults in the UK workforce who lack NVQ2 or equivalent qualifications by 2010. Working towards this, one million adults already in the workforce to achieve Level 2 between 2003 and 2006.	

Health and well-being
Relevant Public Service Agreement 2004 targets

What	Who
Substantially reduce mortality rates by 2010:	DH
• from heart disease and stroke and related diseases by at least 40% in people under 75; with at least a 40% reduction in the inequalities gap between the fifth of areas with the worst health and deprivation indicators and the population as a whole; • from cancer by at least 20% in people under 75, with a reduction in the inequalities gap of at least 6% between the fifth of areas with the worst health and deprivation indicators and the population as a whole; and • from suicide and undetermined injury by at least 20%.	
Reduce health inequalities by 10% by 2010 as measured by infant mortality and life expectancy at birth.	DH

Selected major initiatives under way

Policy	Starting dates	Key department	Key delivery agency	Budget/target/comment
Health Action Zones	1998: first wave 1999: second wave	DH	Health partnerships (NHS, local authorities, voluntary and private sectors)	Aims to improve health and to modernise services in areas of high health need and deprivation. There are 26 zones that will operate for seven years and collectively cover around 13 million people.

Policy	Starting dates	Key department	Key delivery agency	Budget/target/comment
Programme for Action	2003: launched	DH	Health partnerships (NHS, local authorities, voluntary and private sectors)	A plan of action to meet the 2004 Public Service Agreement target to reduce health inequalities.
Modernising Mental Health Services	1999	DH	Health authorities	Aims to reduce mental health problems, including depression. The only specific target is on suicides: to reduce the rate of suicides by at least 20% by 2010.

Low income and work

A household's risk of low income varies greatly depending on how much paid work it does. These risks have increased somewhat for all household types since the mid-1990s.

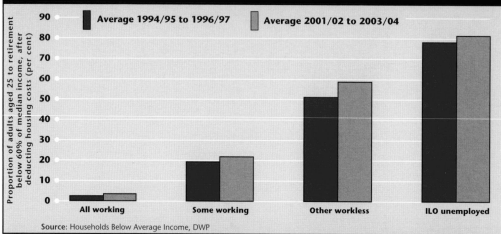

Source: Households Below Average Income, DWP

Among those aged 25 to retirement in low income households, the proportion where the head of the household is unemployed has halved. Almost half now have someone in paid work.

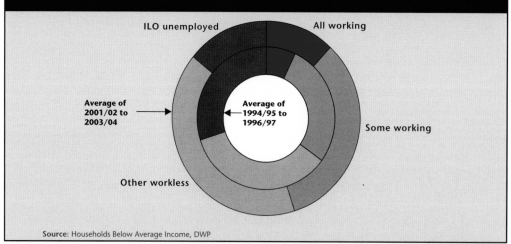

Source: Households Below Average Income, DWP

For people aged 25 to retirement, the first graph shows the risk of a household being on low income, with the data shown separately for the following work statuses: all working (single or couple, with one in full-time work and the other – if applicable – in full-time or part-time work); some working (includes households where no one is working full-time but one or more are working part-time); unemployed (head or spouse unemployed) and other workless (includes long-term sick/disabled and lone parents). The left hand bars show the average for the three years 1994/95 to 1996/97 and the right hand bars show the average for the years 2001/02 to 2003/04.

The second graph shows a breakdown of the low income households by economic status. The inner ring shows the average for the three years 1994/95 to 1996/97 and the outer ring shows the average for the three years 2001/02 to 2003/04. To provide consistency with the first graph, both self-employed households and households where the head or spouse is aged 60 or over are excluded from this analysis.

The data source for both graphs is Households Below Average Income, based on the Family Resources Survey (FRS). The data relates to Great Britain. The averaging over three-year bands has been done to improve the statistical reliability of the results. Income is disposable household income after deducting housing costs. All data is equivalised (adjusted) to account for variation in household size and composition.

Overall adequacy of the indicator: **high**. The FRS is a well-established annual government survey, designed to be representative of the population as a whole.

Low income and disability

Indicator
23

Disabled adults are twice as likely to live in low income households as non-disabled adults, and the gap has grown over the last decade.

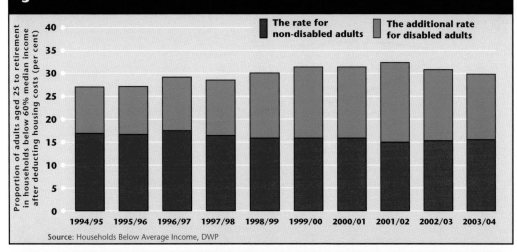

Source: Households Below Average Income, DWP

Disabled people in workless households are somewhat less likely to be in low income than their non-disabled counterparts.

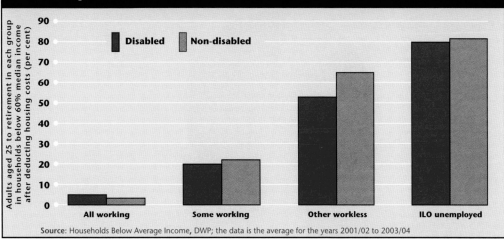

Source: Households Below Average Income, DWP; the data is the average for the years 2001/02 to 2003/04

The first graph shows the proportion of adults aged 25 to retirement living in households below 60% of median income after deducting housing costs, with the data shown separately for disabled and non-disabled adults.

The second graph shows how the risks of being in low income vary by work status, with the data shown separately for disabled and non-disabled working-age adults aged 25 to retirement. The following work statuses are shown: all working (single or couple, with one in full-time work and the other – if applicable – in full-time or part-time work); some working (includes households where no one is working full-time but one or more are working part-time); unemployed (head or spouse unemployed) and other workless (includes long-term sick/disabled and lone parents).

The data source for both graphs is Households Below Average Income, based on the Family Resources Survey (FRS). The data relates to Great Britain. To improve statistical reliability, the data in the second graph is averaged for the years 2001/02 to 2003/04. Income is disposable household income after deducting housing costs. All data is equivalised (adjusted) to account for variation in household size and composition. Where the household contains two adults, one disabled but the other not, and one in the 25 to retirement age group but the other not, it is not possible to tell from the data which of the two adults is disabled. In such cases, the assumption has been made that half of the disabled adults are in the 25 to retirement age group.

Overall adequacy of the indicator: **high**. The FRS is a well-established government survey, designed to be representative of the population as a whole.

Wanting paid work

Indicator 24

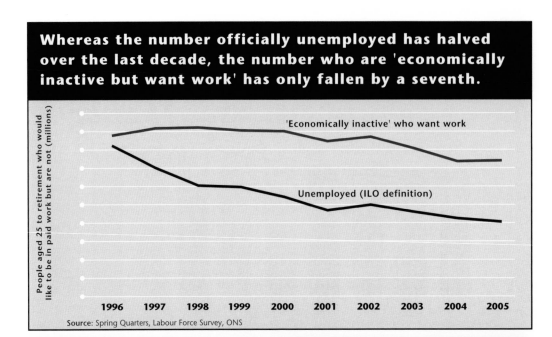

Whereas the number officially unemployed has halved over the last decade, the number who are 'economically inactive but want work' has only fallen by a seventh.

'Economically inactive' who want work

Unemployed (ILO definition)

People aged 25 to retirement who would like to be in paid work but are not (millions)

1996 1997 1998 1999 2000 2001 2002 2003 2004 2005

Source: Spring Quarters, Labour Force Survey, ONS

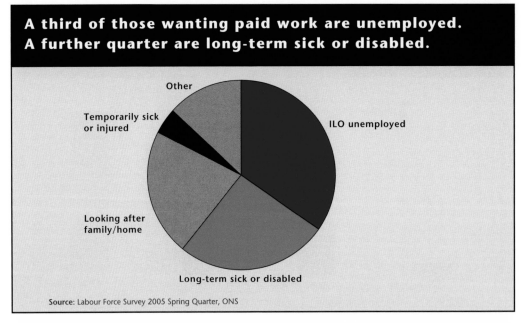

A third of those wanting paid work are unemployed. A further quarter are long-term sick or disabled.

Other

Temporarily sick or injured

ILO unemployed

Looking after family/home

Long-term sick or disabled

Source: Labour Force Survey 2005 Spring Quarter, ONS

The first graph shows the number of people aged 25 to retirement wanting work. It is divided between the unemployed (as defined by the ILO) and those counted as 'economically inactive' who nevertheless want paid work. The data is for the spring quarter of each year.

The second graph shows, for the latest year, the proportions of those aged 25 to retirement who want paid work by reason for their economic inactivity. The data is for the spring quarter of the latest year.

The data source for both graphs is the Labour Force Survey (LFS). The data relates to the United Kingdom. 'Unemployment' is the ILO definition, which is used for the official UK unemployment numbers. It includes all those with no paid work in the survey week who were available to start work in the next fortnight and who either looked for work in the last month or were waiting to start a job already obtained. The economically inactive who want paid work includes people not available to start work for some time and those not actively seeking work. Note that the ILO unemployment rates in these graphs are not the same as in some of the other indicators, as it is percentage of the total population (whereas, in other indicators, it is expressed as a percentage of the economically active population).

Overall adequacy of the indicator: **high**. The LFS is a well-established, quarterly government survey designed to be representative of the population as a whole.

Work and disability

Indicator
25

One in five adults with a work-limiting disability is not working but wants to. This compares with one in fifteen of those with no work-limiting disability.

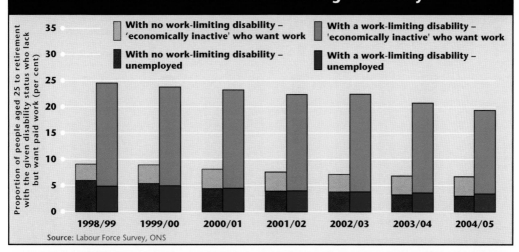

Legend:
- With no work-limiting disability – 'economically inactive' who want work
- With a work-limiting disability – 'economically inactive' who want work
- With no work-limiting disability – unemployed
- With a work-limiting disability – unemployed

Y-axis: Proportion of people aged 25 to retirement with the given disability status who lack but want paid work (per cent)

X-axis: 1998/99, 1999/00, 2000/01, 2001/02, 2002/03, 2003/04, 2004/05

Source: Labour Force Survey, ONS

At all levels of qualification, the proportion of people with a work-limiting disability who lack but want paid work is much greater than for those without a work-limiting disability

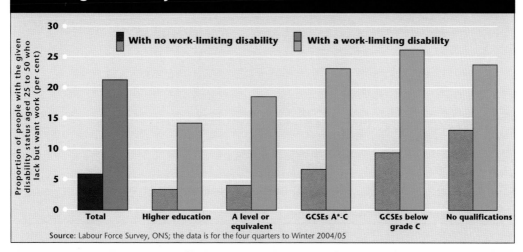

Legend:
- With no work-limiting disability
- With a work-limiting disability

Y-axis: Proportion of people with the given disability status aged 25 to 50 who lack but want work (per cent)

X-axis: Total, Higher education, A level or equivalent, GCSEs A*-C, GCSEs below grade C, No qualifications

Source: Labour Force Survey, ONS; the data is for the four quarters to Winter 2004/05

The first graph shows the proportion of working-age people who are classified as work-limited disabled who lack but want paid work, with the data shown separately for those who are ILO unemployed and 'economically inactive' but want paid work. For comparison purposes, the equivalent data for those with no work-limiting disability is also shown.

The second graph shows how the proportion of those aged 25 to 50 who lack but want paid work (ie those who are ILO unemployed plus those who are economically inactive but want paid work) varies by level of disability and level of highest qualification. To improve statistical reliability, the data is the average for the four quarters to Winter 2004/05.

The data source for both graphs is the Labour Force Survey (LFS) and relates to the United Kingdom. 'Unemployment' is the ILO definition, which is used for the official UK unemployment numbers. It includes all those with no paid work in the survey week who were available to start work in the next fortnight and who either looked for work in the last month or were waiting to start a job already obtained. The economically inactive who want paid work includes people not available to start work for some time and those not actively seeking work. 'Work-limiting disability' is a Labour Force Survey classification and comprises those people who stated that they have had health problems for more than a year and that these problems affect either the kind or amount of work that they can do.

Overall adequacy of the indicator: **high**. The LFS is a large, well-established, quarterly government survey, designed to be representative of the population as a whole.

Workless households

While the number of 2+ adult working-age households who are workless has fallen, the number of single adult households who are workless has not.

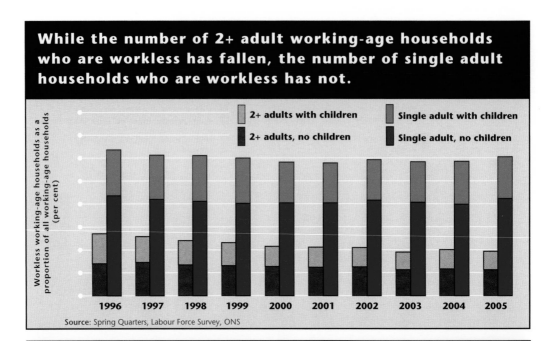

Source: Spring Quarters, Labour Force Survey, ONS

Three-fifths of people in workless working-age households are living in single adult households.

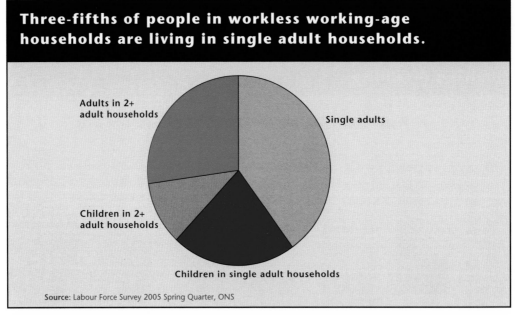

Source: Labour Force Survey 2005 Spring Quarter, ONS

The first graph shows the number of workless working-age households (ie households where none of the adults are working) as a proportion of total working-age households, with the data being grouped into the following four household types: single adults without dependent children, lone parent households, households with two or more adults but no dependent children, and households with two or more adults and one or more dependent children.

The second graph shows, for the latest year, the number of people in workless working-age households in the following four categories: adults in households with only one adult, adults in households with two or more adults, children in households with only one adult and children in households with two or more adults.

The data source for both graphs is the Labour Force Survey (LFS) Household datasets for the spring quarter of each year. Households which are entirely composed of full-time students have been excluded from the analysis, as have households where their economic status is not known. Full-time students have been excluded from the calculations to decide whether the household has one or more than one adult.

Overall adequacy of the indicator: **high**. The LFS is a large, well-established, quarterly government survey, designed to be representative of the population as a whole.

Low pay by gender

Indicator
27

3.7 million female employees aged 22 and over – and 1.8 million male employees aged 22 and over – were paid less than £6.50 per hour in 2004 (equivalent to £5.00 per hour in 1998 after uprating for the average rise in earnings).

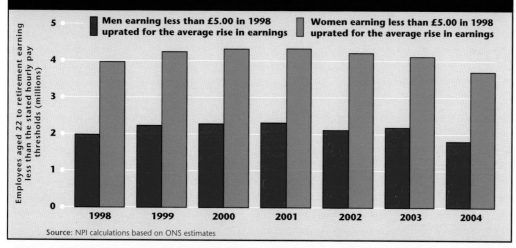

■ Men earning less than £5.00 in 1998 uprated for the average rise in earnings

▨ Women earning less than £5.00 in 1998 uprated for the average rise in earnings

Source: NPI calculations based on ONS estimates

Around half of those paid less than £6.50 per hour are part-time workers, mainly women.

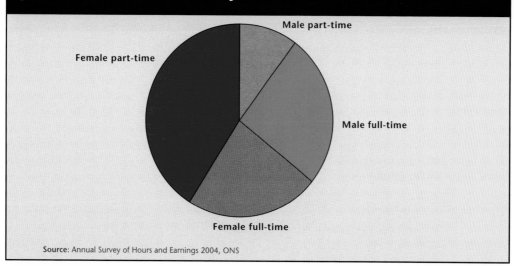

Male part-time

Female part-time

Male full-time

Female full-time

Source: Annual Survey of Hours and Earnings 2004, ONS

The first graph shows the estimated number of employees aged 22 to retirement age who were paid below various hourly rates of pay in each year shown. No data is available for years before 1998 and the available data only distinguishes between the 18 to 21 and 22+ age groups. The low paid threshold used aims to reflect average rise in earnings and rises in line with the ONS Average Earnings Index from a base of £5.00 per hour in 1998. It is therefore £5.22 in 1999, £5.51 in 2000, £5.78 in 2001, £5.95 in 2002, £6.14 in 2003 and £6.46 in 2004. The figures are from published ONS statistics which were themselves derived from a combination of data from the Labour Force Survey (LFS) and Annual Survey of Hours and Earnings (ASHE), with adjustments by the ONS.

The second graph shows, for 2004, the distribution of employees paid less than £6.50 per hour by male/female and full-time/part-time. The data source is the Annual Survey of Hours and Earnings (ASHE). The proportions have been calculated from the hourly rates at each decile using interpolation to estimate the consequent proportion earning less than £6.50 per hour.

Overall adequacy of the indicator: ***medium***. The LFS and ASHE are well-established government surveys, designed to be representative of the population as a whole. However, the ONS methods for combining and adjusting the data are not available for public scrutiny, and the underlying dataset itself is not publicly available. In other words, outside researchers have to rely on whatever data ONS decides to publish.

Low pay by industry

Indicator 28

Around half of employees aged 25 and over in the hotels and restaurants and wholesale and retail sectors earn less than £6.50 per hour. In both sectors, two-thirds of these are women.

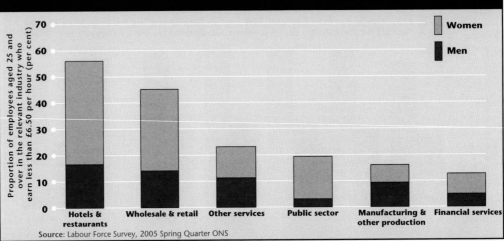

Source: Labour Force Survey, 2005 Spring Quarter ONS

More than a quarter of all employees aged 25 to retirement earning less than £6.50 per hour work in the public sector.

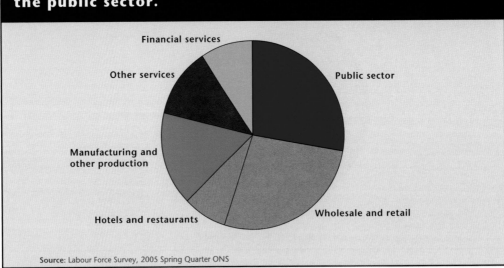

Source: Labour Force Survey, 2005 Spring Quarter ONS

The first graph shows how the proportion of workers aged 25 to retirement who were paid less than £6.50 per hour varies by industry sector, with the data shown separately for men and women.

The second graph shows the share of low paid workers aged 25 to retirement by industrial sector.

The data source for both graphs is the Labour Force Survey Spring Quarter 2005 (equivalent data by age group and industry not being available from the published results of the Annual Survey of Hours and Earnings) and relates to the United Kingdom. People whose hourly pay rates cannot be calculated from the survey data have been excluded from the analysis. Some of the sectors have been combined together for presentational purposes with the particular sectors shown being manufacturing and other production (industry code A-F); wholesale & retail (G); hotels & restaurants (H); public administration, education & health (L-N); other business activities (J-K); and other services (I & O-Q).

Overall adequacy of the indicator: **_medium_**. The Labour Force Survey is a large, well-established, quarterly government survey designed to be representative of the population as a whole but there are some doubts about the reliability of its low pay data.

Low pay and disability

Indicator
29

For both full-time and part-time work, the proportion of employees with a work-limiting disability who are low paid is around 10 per cent higher than that for employees without a work-limiting disability.

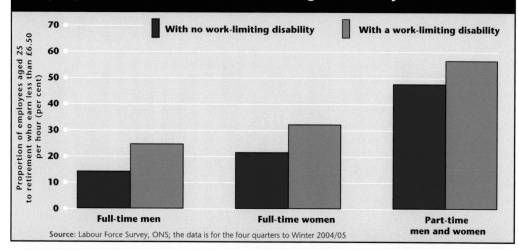

Source: Labour Force Survey, ONS; the data is for the four quarters to Winter 2004/05

At all levels of qualification, the risk of someone with a work-limiting disability being low paid is somewhat higher than that for someone without a work-limiting disability.

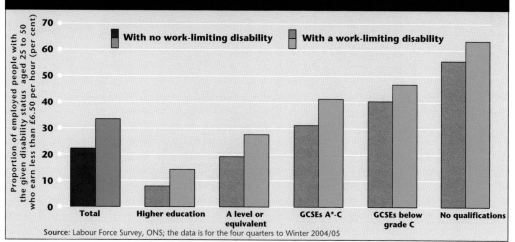

Source: Labour Force Survey, ONS; the data is for the four quarters to Winter 2004/05

The first graph shows how the proportion of workers aged 25 to retirement who were paid less than £6.50 per hour varies by level of disability, gender and full-time/part-time.

The second graph shows how the proportion of workers aged 25 to 50 who were paid less than £6.50 per hour varies by level of disability and level of highest qualification.

The data source for both graphs is the Labour Force Survey (LFS) and relates to the United Kingdom. To improve statistical reliability, the data is the average for the four quarters to winter 2004/05. People whose hourly pay rates cannot be calculated from the survey data have been excluded from the analysis. 'Work-limiting disability' is an LFS classification and comprises those people who stated that they have had health problems for more than a year and that these problems affect either the kind or amount of work that they can do.

Overall adequacy of the indicator: **medium**. The LFS is a large, well-established, quarterly government survey designed to be representative of the population as a whole but there are some doubts about the reliability of its low pay data.

Insecure at work

**Indicator
30**

Almost half of the men, and a third of the women, making a new claim for Jobseeker's Allowance were last claiming less than six months ago. These proportions are similar to a decade ago.

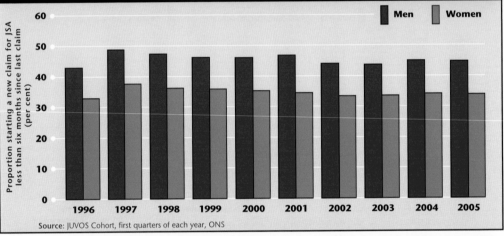

Source: JUVOS Cohort, first quarters of each year, ONS

Only one in twelve part-time employees want a full-time job – but more than a quarter of temporary employees would like a permanent job.

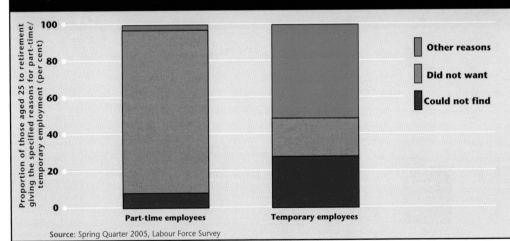

Source: Spring Quarter 2005, Labour Force Survey

The first graph shows the probability that someone who makes a new claim for Jobseeker's Allowance was last claiming that benefit less than six months previously. This is effectively the same as the proportion of people finding work who then lose that work within six months. Figures are shown separately for men and women. The data relates to Great Britain and, for each year, is taken from the first quarter of the Joint Unemployment and Vacancies Operating System (JUVOS) cohort.

The second graph shows data for all employees aged 25 to retirement in part-time and temporary jobs (shown separately) by reason for the part-time or temporary employment. The data source is the 2005 Spring Quarter of the Labour Force Survey. The data relates to the United Kingdom and is not seasonally adjusted.

Overall adequacy of the indicator: **high**. Note, however, that while the claimant count data is sound, the narrow definition of unemployment that it represents means that it understates the extent of short-term working interspersed with spells of joblessness.

Support at work

Although there has been some improvement over the last decade, people with no qualifications are still three times less likely to receive job-related training than those with some qualifications.

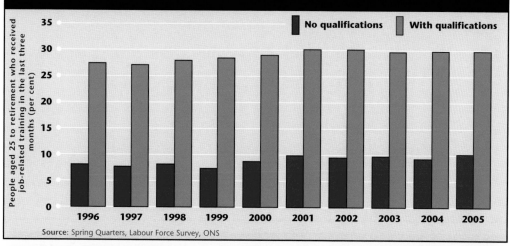

Source: Spring Quarters, Labour Force Survey, ONS

Fifteen per cent of workers earning less than £6.50 an hour belong to a trade union compared with 40 per cent of those earning £9 to £21 an hour.

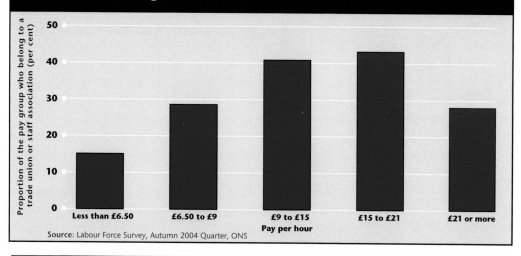

Source: Labour Force Survey, Autumn 2004 Quarter, ONS

The first graph shows the proportion of employees aged 25 to retirement age who have received some job-related training in the previous three months according to whether they have some educational or vocational qualification or not. The qualifications include both current qualifications (eg GCSEs) and qualifications which have been awarded in the past (eg O levels). The data source is the Labour Force Survey (LFS) and the data for each year is from the Spring Quarter. The data relates to the United Kingdom and is not seasonally adjusted. Training includes both that paid for by employers and by employees themselves.

The second graph shows the proportion of people currently employed who are members of a trade union or staff association, with the data shown separately by level of pay. The data source is the 2004 Autumn Quarter of the Labour Force Survey (the data is only collected in the autumn quarters). The data relates to the United Kingdom and is not seasonally adjusted.

Overall adequacy of the indicator: **medium**. The LFS is a well-established, quarterly government survey, designed to be representative of the population as a whole. But a single, undifferentiated notion of 'training,' without reference to its length or nature, lessens the value of the indicator.

Premature death

The rate of premature death fell by a tenth in the decade to 2003. It is, however, still one-and-a-half times as high among men as among women.

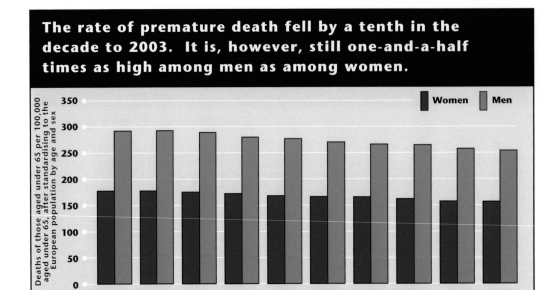

Source: Mortality Statistics Division, ONS

Death rates from heart disease and lung cancer – the two biggest causes of premature death – for people aged 35 to 64 are around twice as high among those from manual backgrounds as from non-manual backgrounds.

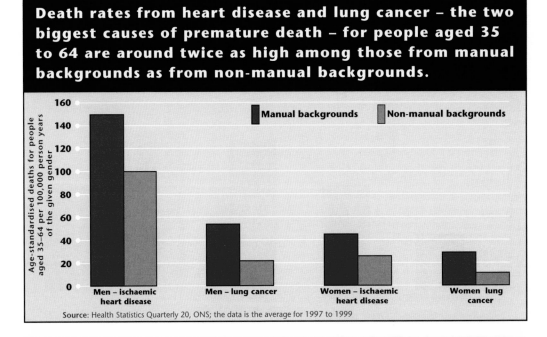

Source: Health Statistics Quarterly 20, ONS; the data is the average for 1997 to 1999

The first graph shows the number of deaths of people aged under 65 per 100,000 population aged under 65, with the data shown separately for males and females. The data source is the Mortality Statistics Division of ONS. The data relates to Great Britain and has been standardised to the European population by both age and gender. The data is actually published at local authority level. To combine the local authority figures to calculate regional figures, the 2001 Census population estimates for the numbers of males and females under 65 have been used as the weighting factors.

The second graph compares death rates among those aged 35 to 64 by social class and gender for the two biggest causes of premature death, namely ischaemic heart disease and lung cancer. The data source is Health Statistics Quarterly 20 (Winter 2003), published by ONS. The data is the average for the years 1997 to 1999 and covers England and Wales. The data is the latest publicly available and the age group is the only one for which published data is available. Each death is coded using the Ninth Revision of the International Classification of Diseases and Related Health Problems (ICD-9). The data for ischaemic heart disease is ICD-9 codes 410 to 414 and that for lung cancers is ICD-9 code 162.

Overall adequacy of the indicator: **high**. The underlying data are deaths organised according to the local authority area of residence of the deceased by the ONS in England and Wales and by the Registrar General for Scotland.

Limiting longstanding illness

A quarter of adults aged 45–64 suffer a longstanding illness or disability which limits their activity.

Indicator
33

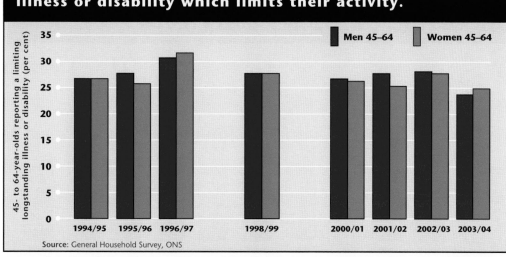

Source: General Household Survey, ONS

Almost half of all adults in the poorest fifth of the population aged 45-64 have a limiting longstanding illness or disability, twice the rate for those on average incomes.

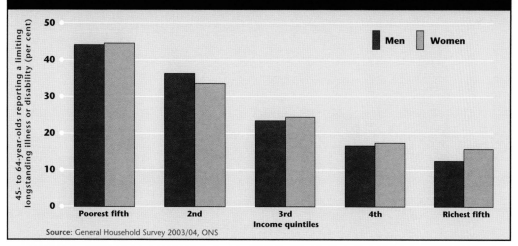

Source: General Household Survey 2003/04, ONS

The first graph shows the proportion of adults aged 45 to 64 who report having a long-term illness or a disability that limits the activities they are able to carry out. The data is shown separately for men and women.

The second graph shows how the proportions for the latest year vary by income. Again, the data is shown separately for men and women.

The data for both graphs is from the General Household Survey (GHS) and relates to Great Britain. The question asked was "Do you have any longstanding illness, disability or infirmity? Longstanding is anything that has troubled you over a period of time or that is likely to affect you over a period of time. Does this illness or disability limit your activities in any way?" Note that the data for 1997 and 1999 is missing because the GHS was not carried out in those years. Also note that the data for 1998/99 onwards is weighted, but for all previous years it is unweighted.

Overall adequacy of the indicator: **medium**. While the GHS is a well-established government survey designed to be representative of the population as a whole, the inevitable variation in what respondents understand and interpret as 'longstanding' and 'limiting activity', diminishes the value of the indicator.

Mental health

Indicator
34

The proportion of adults aged 25 to retirement who are at a high risk of developing a mental illness is similar to a decade ago. Women are more at risk than men.

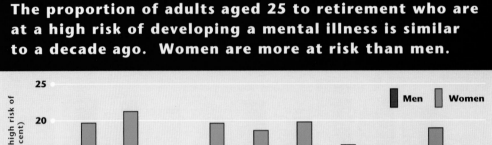

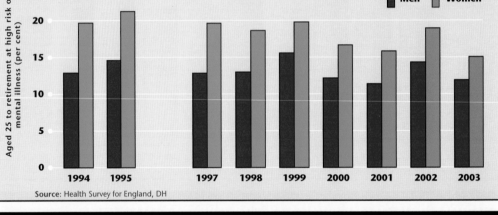

Source: Health Survey for England, DH

Adults in the poorest fifth are twice as likely to be at risk of developing a mental illness as those on average incomes.

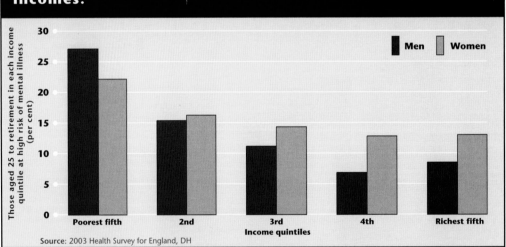

Source: 2003 Health Survey for England, DH

The first graph shows the proportion of adults aged 25 to retirement who are classified as being at high risk of developing a mental illness. This is determined by asking informants a number of questions about general levels of happiness, depression, anxiety and sleep disturbance over the previous four weeks, which are designed to detect possible psychiatric morbidity. A score is constructed from the responses, and the figures published show those with a score of four or more. This is referred to as a 'high GHQ12 score'.

The second graph shows how the proportions for the latest year vary by income, with the data shown separately for men and women.

The data source for both graphs is the Health Survey for England (HSE) and relates to England only. 2003 was the first year that the data was weighted, so the first graph uses unweighted data whilst the second uses weighted data.

Overall adequacy of the indicator: **high**. The HSE is a large survey which is designed to be representative of the population in England as a whole.

5 Pensioners

This chapter has three themes containing seven indicators. The themes are:

- economic circumstances;
- health and well-being;
- isolation and support.

Economic circumstances

Choice of indicators

The first indicator provides information on the degree to which different groups of pensioners have low incomes. The first graph shows these percentages for single pensioners and pensioner couples separately over the last decade. The supporting graph provides further information for single male and female pensioners, as well as pensioner couples, both for those under 75 and those over.

The second indicator focuses on current and future pensioners reliant solely on the state for their income. The first graph shows the number of current pensioners in this situation, separately for single pensioners and couples. The supporting graph shows the proportions of the working population who are not contributing towards a non-state pension, broken down by their current level of income.

The final indicator shows the proportion of pensioners who are entitled to, but not claiming key means-tested benefits, namely the Minimum Income Guarantee (now part of Pension Credit), Housing Benefit and Council Tax Benefit. The first graph shows these proportions annually since the late 1990s while the second reports them separately by tenure.

What the indicators show

Indicator 35 In low income households

All of the fall in the proportion of pensioners in low income households has been among single pensioners rather than pensioner couples.

Older pensioner couples are much more likely to be in low income than younger pensioner couples. The differences are less for single pensioners.

Indicator 36 No private income

1.2 million pensioners have no income other than the state retirement pension and state benefits.

More than half of employees on below-average incomes are not contributing to a non-state pension (although some may belong to a non-contributory pension scheme).

Indicator 37 Non-take-up of benefits

Around two-fifths of pensioner households entitled to Council Tax Benefit are not claiming it, and a third of those entitled to the Minimum Income Guarantee are not claiming it.

Half of all the pensioner households in owner-occupation who were entitled to the Minimum Income Guarantee in 2002/03 did not claim it.

Health and well-being
Choice of indicators

The first indicator shows the extra number of people aged 65 or over who die in the winter months compared with the summer ones. The supporting graph shows the percentage of pensioners who live in energy inefficient housing, separately by tenure and by whether or not they are on low or average incomes for their tenure.

The second indicator relates to pensioners reporting that they suffer from a limiting longstanding illness or disability. The first graph shows the percentages, separately for those under and over age 75, annually since the mid-1990s. The second graph, again comparing those under 75 with those over, shows these percentages according to the pensioner's income level.

What the indicators show
Indicator 38 Excess winter deaths

Each year between 20,000 and 50,000 more people aged 65 or over die in winter months than in other months.

It is owner occupiers and private renters on below average incomes who are the most likely to live in energy inefficient housing.

Indicator 39 Limiting longstanding illness

Two-fifths of adults aged 65 to 74, and half of adults aged 75 and over, report a limiting longstanding illness or disability.

Adults aged 65 to 74 on below average incomes are more likely to have a limiting longstanding illness or disability than those on above average incomes. For those aged 75 and over, this has ceased to be the case.

Isolation and support
Choice of indicators

The first indicator refers to the number of people aged 75 or over who receive home care from their local authority. The first graph shows the proportion helped year by year for a decade, with a division in later years between those receiving intensive help and those receiving non-intensive help only. The supporting graph shows the proportions vary for different types of local authorities, ranging from county councils to inner London boroughs.

The second indicator shows the proportion of people aged 60 or over who report feeling very unsafe out at night. The first graph shows these proportions separately for men and women over the last decade while the supporting graph shows them separately for men and women and by their level of household income.

What the indicators show
Indicator 40 Help to live at home

The number of older people receiving home care has almost halved since 1994 as available resources are increasingly focused on those deemed most in need.

On average, English county councils support fewer older people to live independently at home than either urban or Welsh authorities.

Indicator 41 Anxiety

Among those aged 60 or over, women are three times as likely to feel very unsafe out at night as men.

Women aged 60 and over from lower income households are one-and-a-half times as likely to feel very unsafe out at night as those from higher income households.

Economic circumstances
Relevant Public Service Agreement 2004 targets

What	Who
By 2008, be paying Pension Credit to at least 3.2 million pensioner households, while maintaining a focus on the most disadvantaged by ensuring that at least 2.2 million of these households are in receipt of the Guarantee Credit.	DWP
Improve Housing Benefit administration by:	
• reducing the average time taken to process a Housing Benefit claim to no more than 48 days nationally, and across the bottom 15% of local authorities to no more than 55 days, by March 2008; • increasing the number of cases in the deregulated private rented sector in receipt of Local Housing Allowance to 740,000 by 2008; and • increasing the number of cases in receipt of the Local Housing Allowance where the rent is paid directly to the claimant to 470,000 by 2008.	DWP

Selected major initiatives under way (Also see the Low Income chapter.)

Policy	Starting dates	Key department	Key delivery agency	Budget/target/comment
Winter Fuel Payments (part of Fuel Poverty Initiative)	1997/98: introduced 2000/01: uprated	DWP/HM Treasury	Benefits Agency	Eligible households received £100 in 1999/00, and £200 from 2000/01 onwards, with those aged 80 and over getting £300. Most people aged 60 or over are eligible for payments.
Joint Teams	2004: introduced	DWP	DWP, local authorities and other local service providers	An initiative to improve the coordination of service delivery with an initial focus to increase take-up of entitlements and services. On a case-by-case basis, information will be shared to help identify potential non-claimants of benefits.

Health and well-being
Relevant Public Service Agreement 2004 targets

What	Who
By 2010, bring all social housing into decent condition with most of this improvement taking place in deprived areas; and for vulnerable households in the private sector, including families with children, increase the proportion who live in homes that are in decent condition.	ODPM
Eliminate fuel poverty in vulnerable households in England by 2010 in line with the Government's Fuel Poverty Strategy objective jointly with the Department for Trade and Industry.	DTI and DEFRA

Selected major initiatives under way

Policy	Starting dates	Key department	Key delivery agency	Budget/target/comment
Winter Fuel Payments (part of Fuel Poverty Initiative)	1997/98: introduced 2000/01: uprated	DWP/HM Treasury	Benefits Agency	Eligible households received £100 in 1999/00, and £200 from 2000/01 onwards, with those aged 80 and over getting £300. Most people aged 60 or over are eligible for payments.
UK Fuel Poverty Strategy	2001: launched 2004: updated	DTI/DEFRA	DTI, DEFRA and devolved administrations	Targets: • as far as reasonably practicable, the majority of households living in social sector housing removed from fuel poverty by 2010. • as far as reasonably practicable, no household in Britain should be living in fuel poverty by 2016–18. • substantially increase the number of vulnerable private-sector households living in decent homes by 2010. Budget of £620 million over the period 2005/06 to 2007/08 (including the £140 million for Warm Front below).
Warm Front	May 2000: introduced 2003/04: eligibility criteria widened 2005: second phase commenced	DEFRA	HEES referral networks: local authorities, health bodies and voluntary groups	Previously called the Home Energy Efficiency Scheme. Aims to improve heating and insulation of low income households who are also considered vulnerable (ie with dependent children, pregnant, disabled or aged 60+). From 2003/04, includes central heating for all eligible households. Focused on the private sector. Provides grants of up to £2,500. Average grant of £500. 1 million households in England assisted by the programme by January 2005, with 150,000 of these taken out of fuel poverty. Target of removing 550,000 households from fuel poverty over the period 2005 to 2010. Expenditure of £600 million between 2000 and 2004. Budget of £140 million over 2005 to 2008.
Warm Zones	2001: pilot schemes introduced 2004: pilot schemes completed	DTI and DEFRA	Energy suppliers and other selected partners	Aims to facilitate the efficient, integrated and appropriate delivery of practical measures to alleviate fuel poverty and improve domestic energy efficiency in defined areas. Five pilot schemes with a three year budget of £7 million from a range of sources. The pilot schemes will continue and a limited number of other zones are being established.
Energy Efficiency Commitment	2002: introduced 2004: proposal to continue to at least 2008	DEFRA	Energy suppliers	Requires electricity and gas suppliers to meet targets for domestic energy efficiency and forces them to focus at least half of the resulting activities on low-income consumers. Focused on those in social housing. Ofgem estimates that around 5 million low income households will have benefited by 2005.

Isolation and support

Relevant Public Service Agreement 2004 targets

What	Who
Improve the quality of life and independence of vulnerable older people by supporting them to live in their own homes where possible by: • increasing the proportion of older people being supported to live in their own home by 1% annually in 2007 and 2008; and • increasing by 2008 the proportion of those supported intensively to live at home to 34% of the total of those being supported at home or in residential care.	DH
Tackle social exclusion and deliver neighbourhood renewal, working with departments to help them meet their PSA floor targets, in particular narrowing the gap in health, education, crime, worklessness, housing and liveability outcomes between the most deprived areas and the rest of England, with measurable improvement by 2010.	ODPM
Reassure the public, reducing the fear of crime and anti-social behaviour, and building confidence in the Criminal Justice System without compromising fairness.	Home Office, Department for Constitutional Affairs and Crown Prosecution Service

Selected major initiatives under way

Policy	Starting dates	Key department	Key delivery agency	Budget/target/comment
Better Services for Vulnerable People Initiative	1997: initiated 1999: joint investment plans for older people 2000: extended to all care groups	DH	Health authorities and local authorities jointly	Requires all local and health authorities to draw up Joint Investment Plans to co-ordinate development of services with the aim of ensuring necessary provision while minimising unnecessary admissions to hospitals and care centres.
Community Care (Delayed Discharges) Act 2003	2003	DH	Health authorities and local authorities jointly	Aims to solve the problem of 'bed blocking' by: introducing a financial incentive for local authorities to assess hospital patients' need for community care or carer's services as soon as possible; making intermediate care and certain community equipment services free of charge; ensuring 'seamless care' between local authorities, acute trusts and primary care trusts; and facilitating the move of older people to a more homely environment after hospital treatment as quickly as possible. A 'Building Care Capacity Grant' scheme exists to help with implementation.
Carers' Grant	2002	DH	Local councils	Local councils can use the grant to provide breaks for carers. A budget of around £85 million for England in 2002/03, £100 million in 2003/04 and £185 million in 2005/06.

In low income households

All of the fall in the proportion of pensioners in low income households has been among single pensioners rather than pensioner couples.

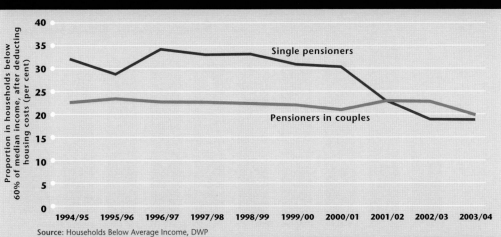

Source: Households Below Average Income, DWP

Older pensioner couples are much more likely to be in low income than younger pensioner couples. The differences are less for single pensioners.

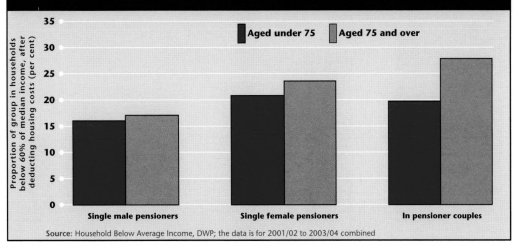

Source: Household Below Average Income, DWP; the data is for 2001/02 to 2003/04 combined

The first graph shows the risk of a pensioner being in a low income household (defined as the proportion of people with incomes below 60% of median household income after deducting housing costs), with the data shown separately for single pensioners and pensioner couples.

The second graph shows the proportion of pensioners living in low income households for different combinations of age group (under 75 and 75 and over) and family type (pensioner couple, single female pensioner and single male pensioner). To improve statistical reliability, the data is averaged for the years 2001/02 to 2003/04.

The data source for both graphs is Households Below Average Income, based on the Family Resources Survey (FRS). The data relates to Great Britain. Income is disposable household income after deducting housing costs. All data is equivalised (adjusted) to account for variation in household size and composition.

Overall adequacy of the indicator: **high**. The FRS is a well-established government survey designed to be representative of the population as a whole. However, since it only covers people living in private households, and not residential institutions (such as nursing homes), it does leave out a significant group of older people.

No private income

Indicator
36

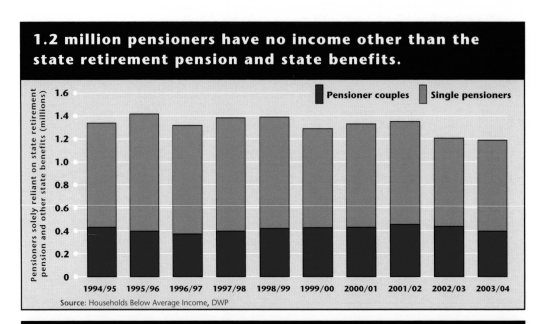

1.2 million pensioners have no income other than the state retirement pension and state benefits.

Pensioners solely reliant on state retirement pension and other state benefits (millions)

■ Pensioner couples   ■ Single pensioners

Source: Households Below Average Income, DWP

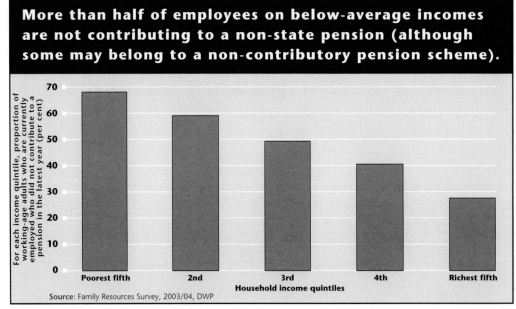

More than half of employees on below-average incomes are not contributing to a non-state pension (although some may belong to a non-contributory pension scheme).

For each income quintile, proportion of working-age adults who are currently employed who did not contribute to a pension in the latest year (per cent)

Poorest fifth   2nd   3rd   4th   Richest fifth

Household income quintiles

Source: Family Resources Survey, 2003/04, DWP

The first graph shows the number of pensioners with no income other than the state retirement pension and state benefits. Note that the figures exclude all those with any other income even if very small. So, for example, the 600,000 pensioners with an additional income of less than £1 per week in 2003/04 are not included in the 2003/04 statistics. The data source is Households Below Average Income, based on the Family Resources Survey (FRS). The data relates to Great Britain (Northern Ireland has been excluded from the figures from 2002/03 onwards as, before this date, FRS only covered Great Britain).

The second graph shows, for the latest year, the proportion of currently employed working-age adults not contributing to a non-state pension, with the data shown separately for each income quintile. Note that 'not contributing to a pension' is not the same as 'not having a pension' because a) some people will belong to a non-contributory pension scheme and b) some people will have a pension which they happen not to have contributed to over the latest year. The data source is FRS. The data relates to the United Kingdom. The income quintiles are defined in terms of disposable household income after deducting housing costs with all data equivalised (adjusted) to account for variation in household size and composition.

Overall adequacy of the indicator: **high**. The FRS is a well-established government survey designed to be representative of the population as a whole. However, since it only covers people living in private households, and not residential institutions (such as nursing homes), it does leave out a significant group of older people.

Non-take-up of benefits

Around two-fifths of pensioner households entitled to Council Tax Benefit are not claiming it, and a third of those entitled to the Minimum Income Guarantee are not claiming it.

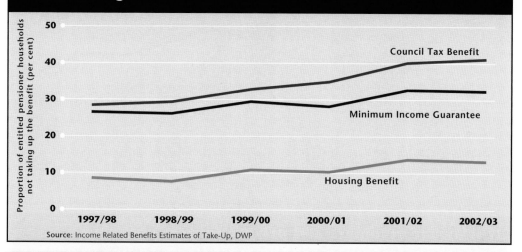

Source: Income Related Benefits Estimates of Take-Up, DWP

Half of all the pensioner households in owner-occupation who were entitled to the Minimum Income Guarantee in 2002/03 did not claim it.

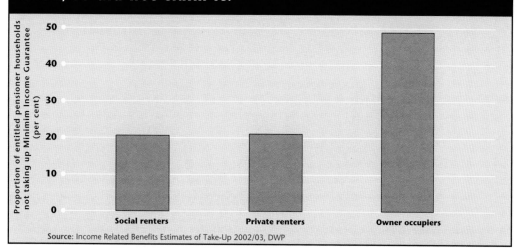

Source: Income Related Benefits Estimates of Take-Up 2002/03, DWP

The first graph shows, for a number of selected benefits, the estimated proportion of pensioner households entitled to the benefit who are not taking up their entitlement. The benefits shown are the three major benefits of older people, namely Council Tax Benefit, Minimum Income Guarantee (now part of Pension Credit) and Housing Benefit. In each case, the estimates are the averages for low end and high end estimates published by DWP.

The second graph shows, for the latest year, the estimated proportion of pensioner households in each housing tenure who are entitled to the Minimum Income Guarantee but are not taking up their entitlement. Equivalent data is not available for either Housing Benefit or Council Tax Benefit.

The data source for both graphs is the Income Related Benefits: Estimates of Take-Up series published by DWP. The data relates to Great Britain. Note that the figures shown are the mid-points of quite wide range estimates, so the figures for any particular benefit in any particular year are subject to considerable uncertainty. So, for example, the proportion of non-take-up of Minimum Income Guarantee for 2002/03 is shown in the first graph as 32% but could be as low as 26% or as high as 38%.

Overall adequacy of the indicator: **medium**. The figures are estimates only, based on the modelling of data from surveys such as the Family Resources Survey.

Excess winter deaths

Indicator
38

Each year between 20,000 and 50,000 more people aged 65 or over die in winter months than in other months.

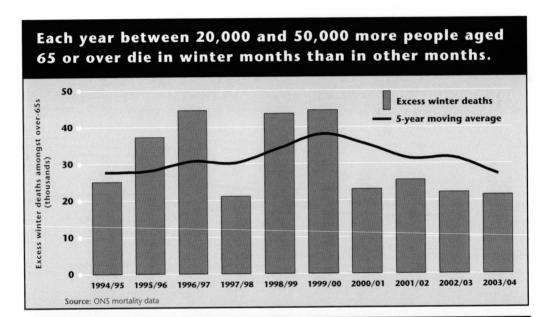

Source: ONS mortality data

It is owner occupiers and private renters on below average incomes who are the most likely to live in energy inefficient housing.

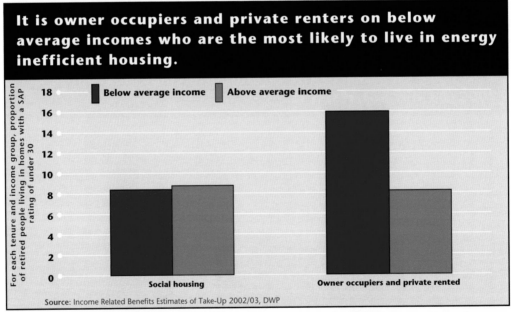

Source: Income Related Benefits Estimates of Take-Up 2002/03, DWP

The first graph shows excess winter deaths each year in the 65 and over age group, where 'excess winter deaths' is defined as the difference between the number of deaths which occurred in winter (December to March) and the average number of deaths during the preceding four months (August to November) and the subsequent four months (April to July). The graph also shows a five-year moving average, which is less affected by year-by-year fluctuations due to particularly cold and warm winters. The data is for England and Wales. The data source is ONS mortality data.

The second graph shows the proportion of retired people who live in homes with a Standard Assessment Procedure (SAP) rating of less than 30, with the data separated out by housing tenure and by level of household income. SAP ratings are a measure of energy efficiency (the higher the SAP rating, the better) ranging from 1 to 100. The threshold of 30 has been used following advice from ODPM. The average incomes used are those which pertain to the particular sector in question (as, otherwise, there would be very few people in social housing on above average incomes). The data source is the 2001 English Household Conditions Survey and the data relates to England.

Overall adequacy of the indicator: **medium**. Whilst the data sources used here are reliable ones, there is no data providing evidence of a direct causal relationship between winter deaths and energy inefficient housing.

Limiting longstanding
illness

Indicator
39

Two-fifths of adults aged 65–74, and half of adults aged 75 and over, report a limiting longstanding illness or disability.

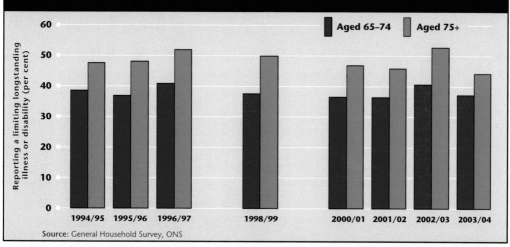

Source: General Household Survey, ONS

Adults aged 65–74 on below-average incomes are more likely to have a limiting longstanding illness or disability than those on above average incomes. For those aged 75 and over, this has ceased to be the case.

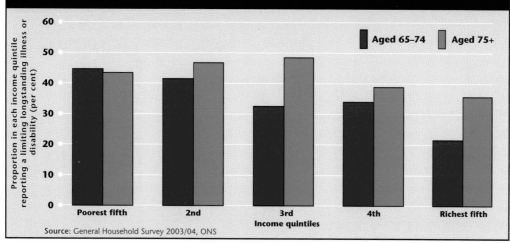

Source: General Household Survey 2003/04, ONS

The first graph shows the proportion of people aged 65 and over who report having a longstanding illness or a disability that limits the activities they are able to carry out. The data is shown separately for those aged 65-74 and those aged 75+.

The second graph shows how the proportions for the latest year vary by income quintile. Again, the data is shown separately for those aged 65-74 and those aged 75+.

The data for both graphs is from the General Household Survey (GHS) and relates to Great Britain. The question asked was "Do you have any longstanding illness, disability or infirmity? Longstanding is anything that has troubled you over a period of time or that is likely to affect you over a period of time. Does this illness or disability limit your activities in any way?" Note that the data for 1997 and 1999 is missing because the GHS was not carried out in those years. Also note that the data for 1998/99 onwards is weighted, but for all previous years it is unweighted.

Overall adequacy of the indicator: **medium**. While the GHS is a well-established government survey designed to be representative of the population as a whole, the inevitable variation in what respondents understand and interpret as 'longstanding' and 'limiting activity', diminishes the value of the indicator.

Help to live at home

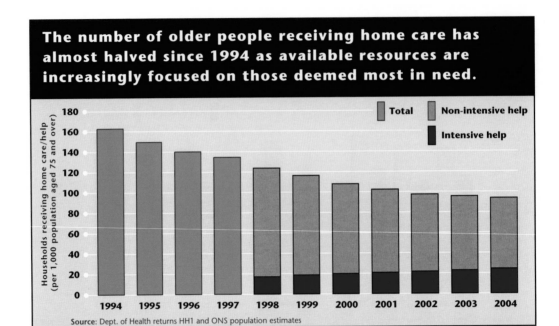

The number of older people receiving home care has almost halved since 1994 as available resources are increasingly focused on those deemed most in need.

Source: Dept. of Health returns HH1 and ONS population estimates

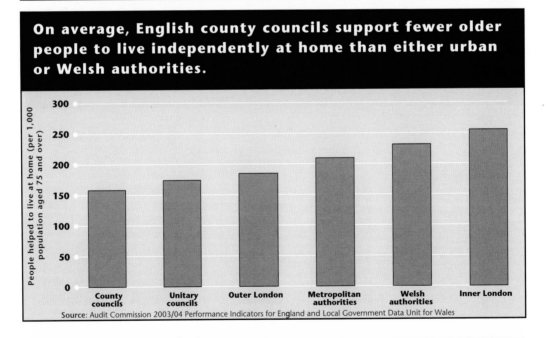

On average, English county councils support fewer older people to live independently at home than either urban or Welsh authorities.

Source: Audit Commission 2003/04 Performance Indicators for England and Local Government Data Unit for Wales

The first graph shows the number of households receiving home help/care from their local authority. The data is expressed per 1,000 population aged 75 and over on the grounds that the majority of people receiving home help/care are in this age group. From 1998 onwards, the data is shown separately for those receiving intensive help (more than 10 hours per week or six or more visits). This division is not available for the earlier years. 'Being helped to live at home' includes provision of the following services: traditional home help services, including home help provided by volunteers; practical services which assist the client to function as independently as possible and/or continue to live in their own homes; and overnight, live-in and 24-hour services. The data source is the Department of Health HH1 returns. The data relates to England. Note that data is collected in a sample week in autumn of the year stated and divided by the estimated population at 30 June in the same year.

The second graph shows how the proportion of people being helped to live at home varies by type of authority. Note that 'being helped to live at home' is a wider measure than the 'receiving home help/care' in the first graph as it includes meals-on-wheels, day care etc. The data source is the Local Government Data Unit for Wales (Wales) and the Audit Commission Best Value Performance Indicators (England). The data is for 2003/04.

Overall adequacy of the indicator: **medium**. The underlying data has been collected for a number of years and can be considered reliable. However, comparisons between local authorities have to be qualified by the fact that statistics ought ideally to be measured in relation to need and levels of support from friends and relatives.

Anxiety

Indicator
41

Among those aged 60 or over, women are three times as likely to feel very unsafe out at night as men.

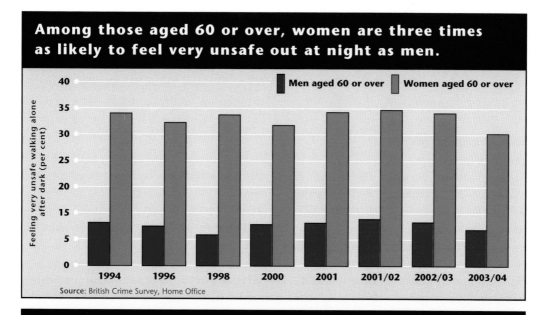

Source: British Crime Survey, Home Office

Among women aged 60 and over, those from lower income households are one-and-a-half times as likely to feel very unsafe out at night as those from higher income households.

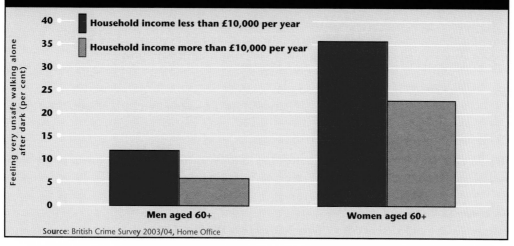

Source: British Crime Survey 2003/04, Home Office

The first graph shows the proportion of people aged 60 or over who say that they feel very unsafe walking alone in their area after dark, with the data shown separately for men and women.

The second graph shows, for the latest year, a breakdown of the statistics according to whether the people lived in households with an annual income of more or less than £10,000.

The data source for both graphs is the British Crime Survey (BCS). The data relates to England and Wales.

Overall adequacy of the indicator: **medium**. The BCS is a well established annual government survey and the fact that the proportions feeling very unsafe have changed little over successive surveys suggests a degree of robustness to this result. However, it is unclear to what extent these feelings reflect anxiety more generally or simply with respect to walking at night.

6 Community

This chapter has three themes containing nine indicators. The themes are:

- social cohesion;
- access to services;
- housing.

Social cohesion
Choice of indicators
The first indicator presents information on the degree to which low income households are concentrated in particular forms of tenure.

The second indicator presents information on the degree to which low income households are concentrated in a relatively small number of local areas.

The third indicator looks both at trends in violent crime and in burglaries and at the degree to which different groups – by tenure, economic status, family type – are likely to be victims of either of these types of crime.

What the indicators show
Indicator 42 Polarisation of low income
Half of all people in social housing are on low incomes compared to one in six of those in other housing tenures.

Almost half of heads of households aged between 25 and 54 in social rented housing are not in paid work compared to just one in twenty of those in owner-occupation.

Indicator 43 Concentrations of low income
Around half of the people on low incomes live in the most deprived fifth of areas. The other half live outside of these areas.

The most deprived fifth of areas have more than three times the proportion of their population on low incomes as other areas.

Indicator 44 Victims of crime
Both burglaries and violent crimes have halved over the last decade.

Lone parent households are more than twice as likely to be burgled as the average household. Unemployed people are three times as likely to be the victims of violence as the average person.

Access to services
Choice of indicators
The first of the indicators here relates to cars, the use that is made of them and the people most likely not to have one. The first graph compares the number of trips made annually by people in households which have cars with the number of trips made by people in households

which do not. The second graph shows the percentage of people by family type, ranging from working-age couples with children, to single pensioners, who do not have a car.

The second indicator shows the percentage of households lacking any type of bank or building society account. The first graph compares low and average income households on this basis over the last decade while the second presents these percentages by ethnic group and economic status.

The third indicator compares the burglary rate over the last five years for households who have home contents insurance with the rate for households who do not. The first graph shows changes over time and the second shows how the percentage lacking such insurance varies according to the level of income.

What the indicators show
Indicator 45 Transport
People in households with a car make more than twice the number of journeys as those without a car.

Just about all working-age couples have a car but many working-age singles – both with and without children – do not.

Indicator 46 Without a bank account
The proportion of low income households with no bank or building society account has fallen substantially in recent years but is still one in six – four times the rate for households on average incomes.

Lone parent, unemployed, sick and disabled and Black households are all around twice as likely to have no account as the average household.

Indicator 47 Without home contents insurance
Households with no insurance cover are three times as likely to be burgled as those with insurance.

Half of the poorest households are uninsured. This compares to one in five for households on average incomes.

Housing
Choice of indicators
The first indicator shows the percentage of households lacking central heating, the first graph comparing low and average income households over the last decade while the supporting graph presents these percentages by household tenure.

The second indicator addresses the problem of homelessness. The first graph shows how many households each year since 1997 have been accepted by their local authority as being 'statutory homeless', the numbers shown separately for households with and without dependent children. People are 'statutory homeless' if they meet both the legal definition of homelessness and have successfully applied to their local authority to be classified as such. The supporting graph shows the various reasons for people becoming homeless and the numbers of homeless households associated with each, with the data perforce only covering those judged to be 'in priority need'.

The final indicator relates to different aspects of insecure owner occupation. The first graph shows the number of mortgage holders in serious arrears each year starting in 1989, that is, before the mortgage crisis in the early 1990s. The second graph shows the number of mortgage holders with either no job or only a part-time job.

What the indicators show
Indicator 48 Without central heating
Although poorer households remain more likely to lack central heating, the proportion who do so is now actually less than that for households on average incomes in 1999/2000.

Those living in the private rented sector are the most likely to be without central heating.

Indicator 49 Homelessness
The number of households without dependent children accepted as homeless has risen sharply in recent years.

By far the biggest reason for becoming homeless is loss of accommodation provided by relatives or friends.

Indicator 50 In mortgage arrears
The number of mortgage holders in serious arrears is at its lowest for 15 years.

One in eight working-age heads of households with a mortgage is in an economically vulnerable position – in part-time work, unemployed or economically inactive.

Social cohesion

Relevant Public Service Agreement 2004 targets

What	Who
Tackle social exclusion and deliver neighbourhood renewal, working with departments to help them meet their PSA floor targets, in particular narrowing the gap in health, education, crime, worklessness, housing and liveability outcomes between the most deprived areas and the rest of England, with measurable improvement by 2010.	ODPM
Reduce crime by 15% and further in high crime areas by 2007/08.	Home Office
Reassure the public, reducing the fear of crime and anti-social behaviour, and building confidence in the Criminal Justice System without compromising fairness.	Home Office, Department for Constitutional Affairs and Crown Prosecution Service

Selected major initiatives under way

Policy	Starting dates	Key department	Key delivery agency	Budget/target/comment
Single Regeneration Budget / Regional Development Agencies Single Programme	1994: introduced, with successive rounds over the years 2001: announcement that there will be no further rounds – subsumed into the Regional Development Agencies Single Programme	ODPM; interdepartmental	Regional Development Agencies (RDAs)	The original objectives were to improve employment prospects, address social exclusion, promote sustainable regeneration, protect the environment and infrastructure, and support and promote economic growth. Under SRB rounds 1–6, 1,000 schemes have been approved worth £5.5 billion in SRB support over their lifetime of up to seven years. From March 2001, RDAs were given more flexibility in the development of their strategies within 11 overall targets (which include a reduction of 10% in the deprivation of those wards that are currently in the bottom 20% of those identified by the Index of Deprivation). As part of this, the various monies for each RDA were pooled.
Employment Zones	1998: initiated 2002: extended to 2004	DfES (DWP also involved)	Partnerships of public, voluntary and private sector organisations	Each zone is situated in an area of high unemployment and aims to get 15–20% improvement in moving selected groups into work. There are 15 zones in total. Government figures are that 50,000 people moved into jobs by March 2005, 80% of which were sustained jobs and 20% lasted less than 13 weeks. Government figures are that Employment Zones had helped 37,000 people into work by May 2003. A budget of £250 million for 1998–2003.

Policy	Starting dates	Key department	Key delivery agency	Budget/target/comment
New Deal for Communities	1998: first round of 17 areas announced 1999: 22 new areas invited to bid for funding 2000: implementation begins in the first round areas 2001: announced there will be no further rounds	ODPM leads a cross-Whitehall initiative	Partnerships of local people, business, community and voluntary organisations and local authorities. RDAs also involved.	An initiative to tackle deprivation in selected areas. Aims to reduce poor job prospects, high levels of crime, educational underachievement and poor health in 39 of the poorest neighbourhoods. Within this, there are a variety of targets including a reduction by a third between 2001 and 2004 in the number of households living in social housing that does not meet defined standards. Each initiative focuses on a small geographic area of up to 4,000 households, with a ten-year timeframe, funding of £20–50 million, and some local flexibility in how the money is spent. England only, with the devolved assemblies/parliaments having their own programmes. A budget of £800 million over 1999–2002, with a ten-year commitment of £2 billion. Government figures point to 7% fewer unemployed residents in New Deal for Communities areas between 2001 and 2003, compared with 5% nationally; pass rates for 5 or more GCSEs A*–C rose by over 5% in New Deal for Communities areas compared with 3.7% England average; and warden areas have seen a decline of nearly 28% in the overall crime rate compared with an increase elsewhere of nearly 5%.
National Strategy for Neighbourhood Renewal	2001: strategy published 2001: Neighbourhood Renewal Unit (NRU) established	NRU leads a cross-Whitehall initiative	Lead government department varies by subject area	Two overall aims: 1. To bridge the gap between the most deprived neighbourhoods and the rest of England. 2. In the worst neighbourhoods to achieve lower long-term worklessness, less crime, better health and better educational qualifications. The strategy includes such schemes as Neighbourhood Renewal Fund, New Deal for Communities, Local Strategic Partnerships, Neighbourhood Management, Street Wardens and Community Chests. A central concept is that of 'floor targets' which no neighbourhood should be below. These floor targets cover the full range of government activity and many are incorporated into the relevant Public Service Agreements (for health, education etc). Budget: funds are divided between various components of NRU. For example: a budget of £900 million to Neighbourhood Renewal Fund from 2001/02 to 2003/04 (for the 88 most deprived wards) and £400 million per year thereafter, £45 million for Neighbourhood Management and £50 million for Community Chest.
Sustainable Communities Plan	2003: launched 2005: updated	ODPM	Partnerships of local people, business, community and voluntary organisations and local authorities. RDAs also involved.	The government's overall programme for delivering sustainable communities. It aims to tackle housing supply issues in the South East, low demand in other parts of the country, and the quality of public spaces. Within this, major elements relate to addressing housing shortages including affordable housing, bringing all social housing up to decent standards by 2010, and improving liveability.

Policy	Starting dates	Key department	Key delivery agency	Budget/target/comment
				The total budget for housing and communities between 2002/03 and 2005/06 is £22 billion of which £5 billion is to regenerate deprived areas, £2.8 billion is to bring council homes up to a decent standard and £200 million is to improve parks and open spaces. A revised government strategy for sustainable communities was published in 2005.
Crime reduction programme	1999: initiated 2002: ended	Home Office	Police and prison service	An umbrella scheme covering 15 separate projects aimed at the Government's general crime reduction targets. A particular target is to reduce domestic burglary by 25% from a 1998/99 baseline, with no local authority area having a rate more than three times the national average by 2005. A budget of £250 million for 2000–2003, with a further £150 million for the CCTV initiative. Local Crime and Disorder Reduction Partnerships now receive direct funding, with a budget of £84 million a year.
Reducing Burglary Initiative	1999: rounds 1 and 2 2000: round 3	Home Office	Local partnerships	Aims to reduce burglary nationally by targeting areas with the worst domestic burglary problems. Round 1 and 2 applicants needed to have a level of burglaries twice the national average and schemes were limited to a duration of one year. Round 3 applicants needed levels of burglaries 1½ times the national average and are of unlimited duration. Between 1999 and 2002, an estimated 2 million homes were covered, preventing an estimated 15,000 burglaries per year. A budget of £25 million over three years.

Access to services

Relevant Public Service Agreement 2004 targets

None identified.

Selected major initiatives under way

Policy	Starting dates	Key department	Key delivery agency	Budget/target/comment
Basic bank accounts	2000: all banks to have such accounts	Treasury	Banks and building societies	Most banks now provide basic bank accounts (no overdraft facilities, but direct debit and cash card available).

Policy	Starting dates	Key department	Key delivery agency	Budget/target/comment
Universal Banking Services	2001: announced 2003: start of rollout	DTI	The Post Office and individual post offices	A joint initiative between the government and the Post Office to provide access to basic bank accounts at post offices. Aims: to modernise welfare payments (ie benefits, pensions and tax credits) by making payments directly into bank accounts, reducing administrative costs and fraud; to increase financial inclusion; and to provide a means of generating replacement business for the Post Office network, helping to ensure it remains viable. From April 2003, benefit payments are being migrated to payment by Automated Credit Transfer (ACT). By the end of the migration period in 2005, it is intended that the normal method of payment will be into a bank account. Also envisages people being able to access their basic bank accounts at post offices. Major banks expected to contribute up to £180 million to the cost of running the post office accounts.

Housing
Relevant Public Service Agreement 2004 targets

What	Who
By 2010, bring all social housing into decent condition with most of this improvement taking place in deprived areas, and for vulnerable households in the private sector, including families with children, increase the proportion who live in homes that are in decent condition.	ODPM
Eliminate fuel poverty in vulnerable households in England by 2010 in line with the Government's Fuel Poverty Strategy objective joint with the Department for Trade and Industry.	DTI and DEFRA
Achieve a better balance between housing availability and the demand for housing, including improving affordability in all English regions while protecting valuable countryside around our towns, cities and in the green belt and the sustainability of towns and cities.	ODPM
By 2010, bring all social housing into decent condition with most of this improvement taking place in deprived areas, and for vulnerable households in the private sector, including families with children, increase the proportion who live in homes that are in decent condition.	ODPM

Selected major initiatives under way

Policy	Starting dates	Key department	Key delivery agency	Budget/target/comment
Winter Fuel Payments (part of Fuel Poverty Initiative)	1997/98: introduced 2000/01: uprated	DWP/HM Treasury	Benefits Agency	Eligible households received £100 in 1999/00, and £200 from 2000/01 onwards, with those aged 80 and over getting £300. Most people aged 60 or over are eligible for payments.

Policy	Starting dates	Key department	Key delivery agency	Budget/target/comment
UK Fuel Poverty Strategy	2001: launched 2004: updated	DTI/DEFRA	DTI, DEFRA and devolved administrations	Targets: • As far as reasonably practicable, the majority of households living in social sector housing removed from fuel poverty by 2010. • As far as reasonably practicable, no household in Britain should be living in fuel poverty by 2016–18. • Substantially increase the number of vulnerable private sector households living in decent homes by 2010. Budget of £620 million over the period 2005/06 to 2007/08 (including the £140 million for Warm Front below).
Warm Front	May 2000: introduced 2003/04: eligibility criteria widened 2005: second phase commenced	DEFRA	HEES referral networks: local authorities, health bodies and voluntary groups	Previously called the Home Energy Efficiency Scheme. Aims to improve heating and insulation of low income households who are also considered vulnerable (ie with dependent children, pregnant, disabled or aged 60+). From 2003/04, includes central heating for all eligible households. Focused on the private sector. Provides grants of up to £2,500. Average grant of £500. 1 million households in England assisted by the programme by January 2005, with 150,000 of these taken out of fuel poverty. Target of removing 550,000 households from fuel poverty over the period 2005 to 2010. Expenditure of £600 million between 2000 and 2004. Budget of £140 million over 2005 to 2008.
Warm Zones	2001: pilot schemes introduced 2004: pilot schemes completed	DTI and DEFRA	Energy suppliers and other selected partners	Aims to facilitate the efficient, integrated and appropriate delivery of practical measures to alleviate fuel poverty and improve domestic energy efficiency in defined areas. Five pilot schemes with a three year budget of £7 million from a range of sources. The pilot schemes will continue and a limited number of other zones are being established.
Energy Efficiency Commitment	2002: introduced 2004: proposal to continue to at least 2008	DEFRA	Energy suppliers	Requires electricity and gas suppliers to meet targets for domestic energy efficiency and forces them to focus at least half of the resulting activities on low-income consumers. Focused on those in social housing. Ofgem estimates that around 5 million low income households will have benefited by 2005.
Housing Investment Programme (HIP) reforms	Gradual	ODPM	Local authorities	A variety of targets including: (1) By March 2002, to reduce the backlog of council house repairs by at least 250,000 with more than 1½ million council houses benefiting from the new investment by March 2002. (2) To reduce the number of people sleeping rough by two-thirds from current levels by 2002 (achieved).

Policy	Starting dates	Key department	Key delivery agency	Budget/target/comment
				An overall budgetary allocation of £2.65 billion in 2001/02 and £2.55 billion in 2002/03. From 2002/03, HIP became part of the Single Capital Pot process whereby the bulk of capital resources are allocated to local authorities through a cross-service Basic Credit Approval.
The capital receipts initiative to release council house sale monies	1997	ODPM	Local authorities	Aims include tackling poor housing and poor health in run down estates. A budget of £1.3 billion over the three years to 1999/00.
Supporting People Programme	2003	ODPM	Working partnership of service users, support agencies and local authorities, NHS and probation services	Aims to improve housing-related support services for vulnerable people (including victims of domestic violence, older people and teenage parents) including those who might be at risk of homelessness. The type of provision offered includes housing management, housing-related support (such as independent living skills), home care, meals services and personal care. Budget of £1.8 billion for 2004/05. An estimated 250,000 units of housing-related support, compared to 100,000 in 2000.
Homelessness Act 2002	2002	ODPM	Local authorities, housing authorities, and social services authorities	Aims to improve both the provision for those who are homeless (primarily by extending local authorities' duty to provide housing to a larger group of homeless people) and the quality and coherence of preventative work (through the introduction of a statutory duty on local authorities to conduct homelessness reviews and compile homelessness strategies). At around the same time, the Homelessness Directorate was formed, bringing together the Rough Sleepers Unit and the Bed-and-Breakfast Unit.
Housing Act 2004	2004	ODPM	Local authorities, housing authorities	Aims to protect the most vulnerable in society and help to create a fairer and better housing market.
Housing strategy	2005	ODPM	Local authorities, housing authorities	The government's housing strategy, with its aims including more opportunities for home ownership, better housing and services for those who rent, and secure housing for the homeless.
Homelessness strategy	2005	ODPM	Local authorities, housing authorities	The government's homelessness strategy. Includes the target of halving the number of households in temporary accommodation by 2010. Hostel provision for homeless people will also be one of the six priority areas for the new Invest to Save – Inclusive Communities fund, worth £90 million in total.

Polarisation of low income

Indicator
42

Half of all people in social housing are on low incomes compared to one in six of those in other housing tenures.

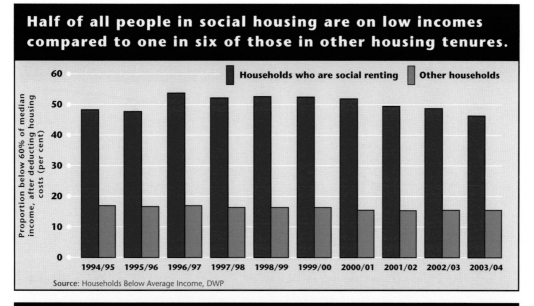

Source: Households Below Average Income, DWP

Almost half of heads of households aged between 25 and 54 in social rented housing are not in paid work compared to just one in twenty of those in owner-occupation.

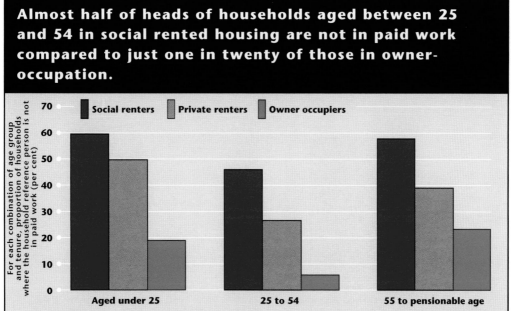

Source: 2001 Census

The first graph shows the proportion of people in low income households for people in social housing compared to people in other housing tenures. The data source is Households Below Average Income, based on the Family Resources Survey (FRS). The data relates to Great Britain. Income is disposable household income after deducting housing costs. All data is equivalised (adjusted) to account for variation in household size and composition. The self-employed are included in the calculations.

The second graph shows the proportion of working-age households where the 'household reference person' (which is the person with the highest income in the household) is not in paid work, with the data broken down by age group and tenure. The data source is the 2001 Census. The data relates to the United Kingdom.

Overall adequacy of the indicator: **high**. The FRS is a well-established annual government survey, designed to be representative of the population as a whole.

Concentrations of low income

Indicator
43

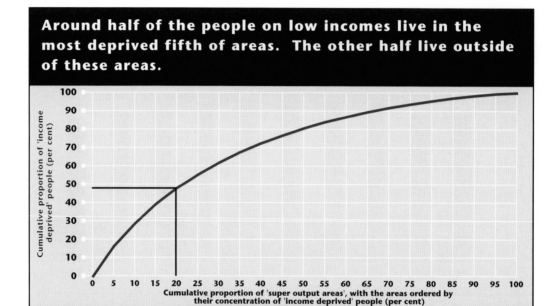

Around half of the people on low incomes live in the most deprived fifth of areas. The other half live outside of these areas.

Source: Index of Deprivation 2004, mostly 2001 data

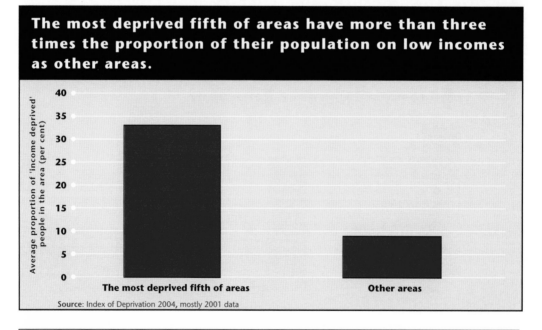

The most deprived fifth of areas have more than three times the proportion of their population on low incomes as other areas.

Source: Index of Deprivation 2004, mostly 2001 data

The first graph shows the extent to which people on low incomes are concentrated in particular geographic areas. The Index of Deprivation 2004 divides England into a large number of 'super output areas zones', each of which is a small geographic area (England is divided into 32,500 super output areas) and provides estimates for the number of 'income deprived' people in each of these data zones. Note that the numbers of 'income deprived' people is not the same definition as the definition of low income used elsewhere. In the graph, the horizontal axis is the cumulative proportion of data zones, ordered by their concentration of 'income deprived' people. The vertical axis is the cumulative proportion of 'income deprived' people, So, for example, the graph shows that 48% of 'income deprived' people are in the fifth of areas with the highest concentrations of such people.

The second graph show the proportion of people who are 'income deprived' in both the fifth of areas with the highest concentrations of such people and the other four-fifths of areas.

The data source for both graphs is the 2004 Index of Deprivation.

Overall adequacy of the indicator: ***medium***. Whilst the underlying data in the Index of Deprivation is not available, it is clearly based on extensive data from the Department of Work and Pensions and Inland Revenue. However, many poor sick and disabled people are excluded from the count because those responsible for constructing the Index of Deprivation decided to exclude those in receipt of Incapacity Benefit on the grounds that it is contributory rather than means-tested.

Victims of crime

Indicator
44

Both burglaries and violent crimes have halved over the last decade.

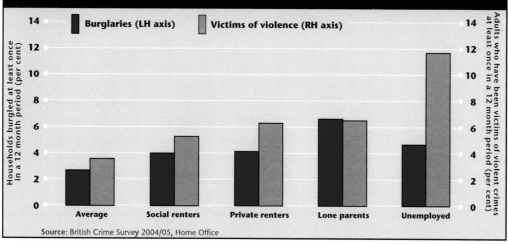

Legend: ■ Burglaries ■ Violence with injury

Y-axis: Number of incidents (millions)

X-axis: 1995, 1997, 1999, 2001/02, 2002/03, 2003/04, 2004/05

Source: British Crime Survey, Home Office

Lone parent households are more than twice as likely to be burgled as the average household. Unemployed people are three times as likely to be the victims of violence as the average person.

Legend: ■ Burglaries (LH axis) ■ Victims of violence (RH axis)

Left Y-axis: Households burgled at least once in a 12 month period (per cent)

Right Y-axis: Adults who have been victims of violent crimes at least once in a 12 month period (per cent)

X-axis: Average, Social renters, Private renters, Lone parents, Unemployed

Source: British Crime Survey 2004/05, Home Office

The first graph shows the number of burglaries and violent incidents with injury in each year shown.

The second graph shows, for the latest year, how the risk of burglary and violent incidents varies for selected groups. Note that burglary is a crime against a household so the figures are presented as a proportion of households whereas violent crime is a crime against the individual so the figures are presented as a proportion of adults. This difference also restricts the number of groups for which data on both burglaries and violent crime exists. Finally, note that the 'unemployed' status for burglaries is where the household reference person is unemployed.

The data source for both graphs is the British Crime Survey (BCS). The data is for England and Wales (BCS only covers England and Wales). In the period up to the year 2000, the BCS survey was undertaken every two years, in the even-numbered years. Whereas the views that people expressed applied to those years, the crimes that they report refer to the previous odd-numbered year. From 2001/02, BCS became an annual survey with the data on both views and crimes relating to the year of each survey.

Overall adequacy of the indicator: **high**. BCS is a well-established government survey, which is designed to be nationally representative.

Transport

Indicator
45

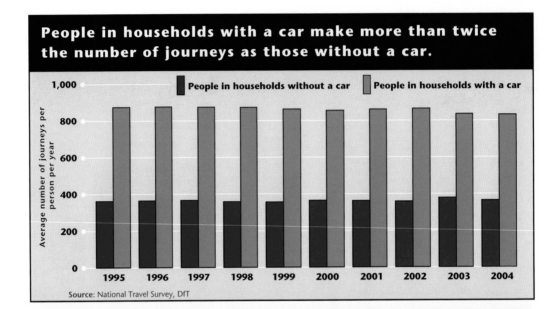

People in households with a car make more than twice the number of journeys as those without a car.

■ People in households without a car ■ People in households with a car

Average number of journeys per person per year

1995 1996 1997 1998 1999 2000 2001 2002 2003 2004

Source: National Travel Survey, DfT

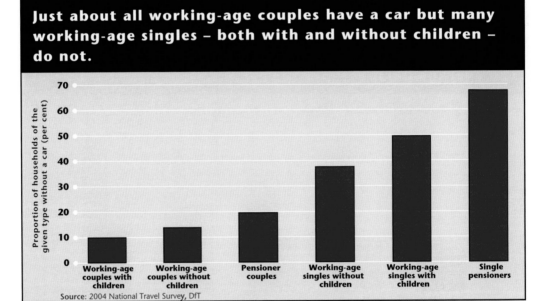

Just about all working-age couples have a car but many working-age singles – both with and without children – do not.

Proportion of households of the given type without a car (per cent)

Working-age couples with children | Working-age couples without children | Pensioner couples | Working-age singles without children | Working-age singles with children | Single pensioners

Source: 2004 National Travel Survey, DfT

The first graph shows the average number of journeys made by people each year, with the data split between those in households with and without cars. The data source is the National Travel Survey and the data relates to Great Britain. The number of journeys has been calculated as the total number of trips by all methods less the number of walking trips.

The second graph shows, for the latest year, the proportion of households who do not have access to either a car or van, with the data shown separately for each major type of household.

The data source for both graphs is the National Travel Survey and the data relates to Great Britain. Households are classified as working-age or pensioner depending on whether the household reference person is aged 65+ or not. Up until 2001, The National Travel Survey results were published on a three-year rolling basis. Following advice from the Department for Transport, the individual year estimates have been made by applying the three-year averages to the middle year of the three (eg the figures for 2000 are those for the three-year period from 1999 to 2001). Figure for 2001 cannot be estimated on this basis so the figures shown are the average for the years 2000 and 2002.

Overall adequacy of the indicator: *medium*. The National Travel Survey is a well-established annual government survey, designed to be nationally representative, but it is not at all clear that the data fully captures the problems of transport in relation to poverty and social exclusion.

Without a bank account

Indicator
46

The proportion of low income households with no bank or building society account has fallen substantially in recent years but is still one in six – four times the rate for households on average incomes.

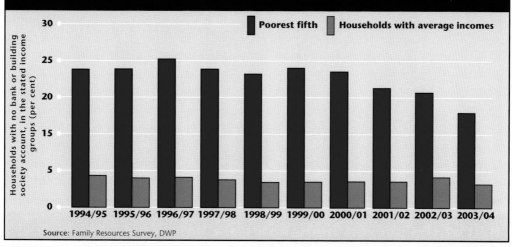

Source: Family Resources Survey, DWP

Lone parent, unemployed, sick and disabled and Black households are all around twice as likely to have no account as the average household.

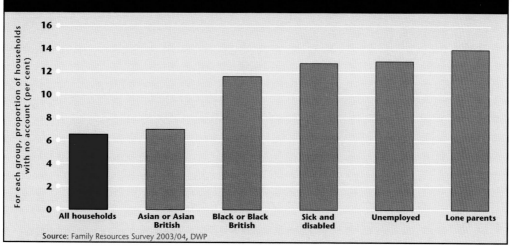

Source: Family Resources Survey 2003/04, DWP

The first graph shows the proportion of households without a bank, building society or any other kind of account. The data is split to show households in the poorest fifth of the income distribution and for households on average incomes (middle fifth of the income distribution) separately. Income is household disposable income, equivalised (adjusted) to take account of household composition and is measured after deducting housing costs.

The second graph shows how the proportions in the latest year vary for selected different household types, as determined by the head of the household. A figure for all households is provided for comparison.

The data source for both graphs is the Family Resources Survey (FRS). The data relates to Great Britain in the first graph and to the United Kingdom in the second graph (FRS did not cover Northern Ireland prior to 2002/03). As well as bank, building society and post office accounts, the figures also count any savings or investment accounts but do not include stocks and shares, premium bonds, gilts or Save As You Earn arrangements.

Overall adequacy of the indicator: **high**. FRS is probably the most representative of the surveys that gather information on the extent to which people have bank and other types of account.

Without home contents insurance

Indicator 47

Households with no insurance cover are three times as likely to be burgled as those with insurance.

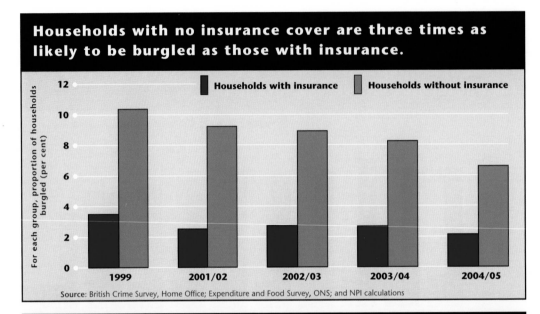

Source: British Crime Survey, Home Office; Expenditure and Food Survey, ONS; and NPI calculations

Half of the poorest households are uninsured. This compares to one in five for households on average incomes.

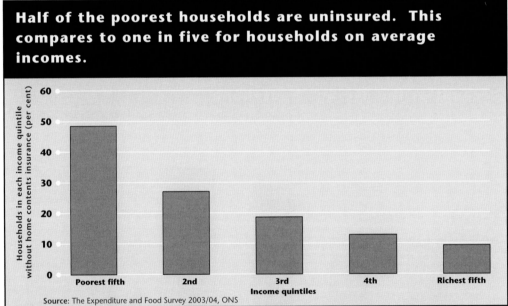

Source: The Expenditure and Food Survey 2003/04, ONS

The first graph shows the proportion of households with, and without, home contents insurance that were victims of a burglary one or more times in each of the years shown. The rate is calculated by the New Policy Institute using data on burglaries from the British Crime Survey (BCS) and data on household insurance from the Expenditure and Food Survey (EFS). The estimates are for England and Wales. Note that data for years earlier than 1999 has not been included in the graph as it was collected on a different basis (via a direct question in the BCS) and is therefore not directly comparable.

The second graph shows, for the year 2003/04, how the proportion of households without insurance cover for household contents varies according to the household's income . The division into income quintiles is based on gross, non-equivalised income. The data source is EFS and relates to the United Kingdom.

Overall adequacy of the indicator: *medium*. The BCS and EFS are well-established government surveys, which are designed to be nationally representative.

Without central heating

Indicator
48

Although poorer households remain more likely to lack central heating, the proportion who do so is now actually less than that for households on average incomes in 1999/00.

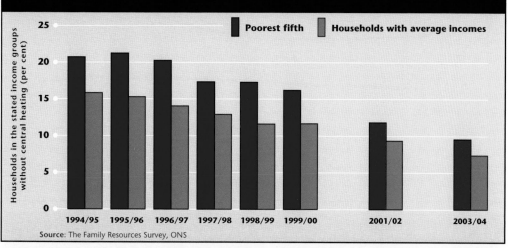

Source: The Family Resources Survey, ONS

Those living in the private rented sector are the most likely to be without central heating.

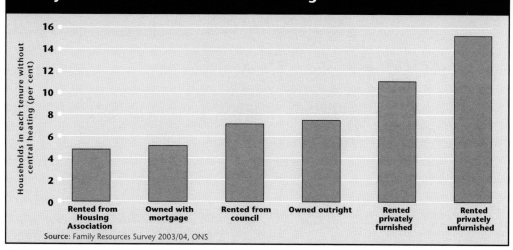

Source: Family Resources Survey 2003/04, ONS

The first graph shows the proportion of households without central heating. The data is split to show households in the poorest fifth of the income distribution and for households on average incomes (middle fifth of the income distribution) separately. Income is household disposable income, equivalised (adjusted) to take account of household composition and is measured after deducting housing costs.

The second graph shows, for the latest year, how the proportion varies by housing tenure.

The data source for both graphs is the Family Resources Survey (FRS). The data relates to Great Britain in the first graph and to the United Kingdom in the second graph (FRS did not cover Northern Ireland prior to 2002/03). The missing years in the first graph are because the question about central heating is only asked in some years.

Overall adequacy of the indicator: **high**. The FRS is a well-established, regular government survey, designed to be nationally representative.

Homelessness

Indicator
49

The number of households without dependent children accepted as homeless has risen sharply in recent years.

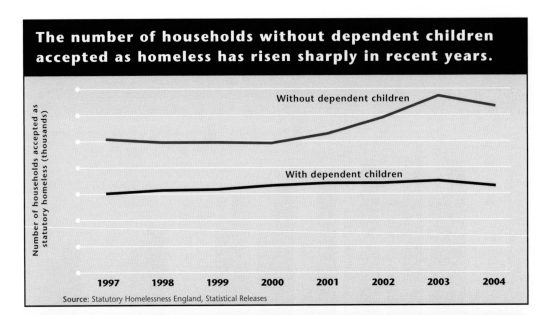

Source: Statutory Homelessness England, Statistical Releases

By far the biggest reason for becoming homeless is loss of accommodation provided by relatives or friends.

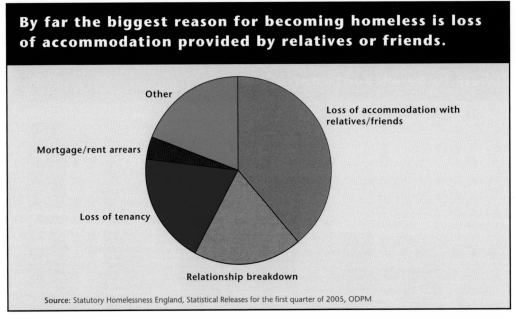

Source: Statutory Homelessness England, Statistical Releases for the first quarter of 2005, ODPM

The first graph shows the number of households in England who are accepted as statutory homeless by their local authority in each of the stated years, with the data split between those with and without dependent children. It includes both those 'in priority need' and those 'not in priority need' but excludes those deemed to be intentionally homeless (a relatively small number). In line with ODPM guidance, the numbers with children are assumed to be the same as the numbers who are in priority need because they have children. Scotland and Wales are not included in this graph because the legislative environment is different.

The second graph provides, for the first quarter of 2005, a breakdown of the households that were accepted by local authorities in England as being homeless and 'in priority need' (no equivalent statistics are kept for those 'not in priority need') according to the reason why the household became homeless.

Overall adequacy of the indicator: **limited**. While there is no reason to believe there is any problem with the underlying data, the extent to which it leaves 'homelessness' dependent on administrative judgement is not satisfactory. In particular, the figures do not include many single people who are effectively homeless, as local authorities have no general duty to house such people and therefore many do not apply.

In mortgage arrears

Indicator
50

The number of mortgage holders in serious arrears is at its lowest for fifteen years.

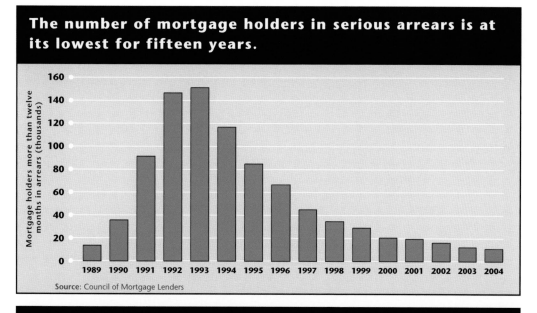

Source: Council of Mortgage Lenders

One in eight working-age heads of households with a mortgage is in an economically vulnerable position – in part-time work, unemployed or economically inactive.

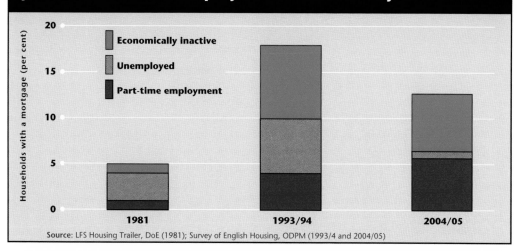

Source: LFS Housing Trailer, DoE (1981); Survey of English Housing, ODPM (1993/4 and 2004/05)

The first graph shows the number of residential mortgage holders who were 12 months or more in arrears with their mortgage repayments at the end of each of the years shown. The data is from the Council of Mortgage Lenders (CML) and relates to the United Kingdom. The figures are based on a sample which typically averages 85% of the total mortgage market in any given year.

The second graph shows the proportion of households with mortgages where the head of the household has the economic status shown. The data is from the Survey of English Housing and relates to England only.

Overall adequacy of the indicator: **high**. The data for the first graph is produced regularly by the CML from surveys among their members. The data for the second graph is from a well-established government survey designed to be nationally representative.

7 Maps

This chapter provides a number of maps showing how the prevalence of some of the indicators from the earlier chapters varies by local authority area.

The first four maps relate to Great Britain and the second four relate to England. There are no separate maps for either Scotland or Wales as these are included in separate Scottish and Welsh reports.

GB maps

Choice of maps

The four maps cover:

- working-age recipients of out-of-work benefits (see indicator 24);
- older recipients of benefits – i.e. the guaranteed part of Pension Credit (see indicator 35);
- low pay (see indicator 27);
- premature death (see indicator 32).

In each case, the data is at local authority district level, with the districts with above average prevalence shaded and those with below-average prevalence not shaded.

What the maps show

The pattern of dependence on social security benefits among working-age people is largely similar to the pattern of dependence among pensioners, with urban, rural and coastal areas all figuring in the list of the most dependent.

Low pay is most widespread in rural parts of England, mid and west Wales, and southern Scotland. London, the northern cities and Glasgow/Edinburgh all have below average proportions of low pay.

Every part of Scotland has rates of premature death above the GB average. Elsewhere, rates are highest in the inner cities and parts of South Wales.

England maps

Choice of maps

The four maps cover:

- failure to obtain five or more GCSEs (see indicator 14);
- underage pregnancies (see indicator 12);
- older people not being helped to live at home (see indicator 40);
- homelessness (see indicator 49).

These maps are for England only because the data for England, Scotland and Wales is not directly comparable. In the first three cases, the data is at local authority upper tier level, with that for homelessness being at lower tier (district) level. Areas with above average prevalence are shaded and those with below average prevalence are not shaded.

What the maps show

Both underage pregnancies and failure to obtain five or more GCSEs are most common in urban areas and, with some exceptions, follow similar patterns.

The local authorities who help the fewest of their older citizens to live at home are outside of the cities, across southern England, East Anglia and Yorkshire.

Though worst in London and the North East, both rural and urban areas anywhere in the country can have serious problems of homelessness.

**Reliant on benefits:
working age**

**Reliant on benefits:
older people**

Low pay

Premature death

| ■ Highest sixth | ■ Next sixth | ■ Third sixth | □ Below average |

Great Britain maps

Reliant on benefits – working age
Urban, rural and coastal areas all figure in the list of the local authorities with the highest rates of working-age reliance on out-of-work benefits.

The map shows how the proportion of working-age people claiming one or more 'key out-of-work benefits' varies by local authority. 'Key out-of-work benefits' is a DWP term which covers the following benefits: Jobseeker's Allowance, Income Support, Incapacity Benefit and Severe Disablement Allowance.

The data source is the DWP Information Centre and the data is for February 2005. The data has been analysed to avoid double-counting of those receiving multiple benefits by matching data from individual samples.

Reliant on benefits: older people
With some exceptions, the pattern for the local authority areas with the highest rates of pensioner reliance on benefits are generally similar to those for working-age reliance on benefits.

The map shows how the proportion of people in receipt of the 'guaranteed' part of Pension Credit (previously called the Minimum Income Guarantee) varies by local authority, thus providing an indication of how the prevalence of low income among older people varies by local authority.

The data source is the DWP Information Centre and the data is for February 2005.

Low pay
Low pay is most widespread in rural parts of England, mid- and west-Wales, and southern Scotland. London, the northern cities and Glasgow/Edinburgh all have below average proportions of low pay.

The map shows, for 2004, how the proportion of employees paid less than £6.50 per hour varies by local authority.

The data source is the Annual Survey of Hours and Earnings (ASHE) including the supplementary data for non-VAT companies. The data includes both full-time and part-time employees. The proportions have been calculated from the hourly rates at each decile using interpolation to estimate the consequent proportion earning less than £6.50 per hour.

Premature death
Every part of Scotland has rates of premature death above the GB average. Elsewhere, rates are highest in the inner cities and parts of South Wales.

The map shows how the proportion of the population aged under 65 who died varies by local authority. Note that small sample sizes mean that each authority's figures will be subject to some uncertainty and, to improve statistical reliability, the data is averaged over the years 2001 to 2003.

The data source is the Mortality Statistics Division of ONS. The data has been standardised to the European population by both age and sex.

Failing to obtain 5 or more GCSEs

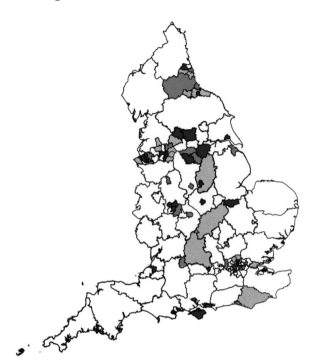

Underage pregnancies

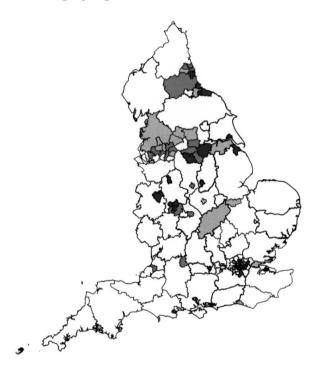

Older people not being helped to live at home

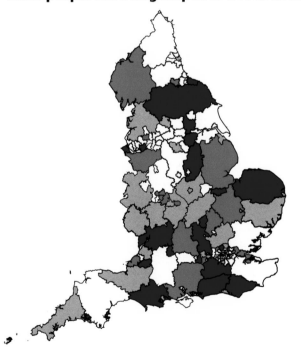

Homelessness

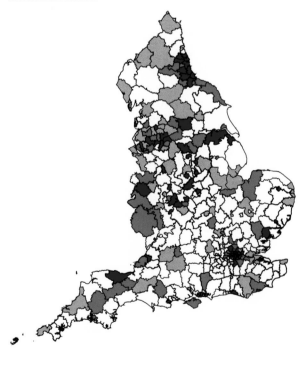

■ Highest sixth　　■ Next sixth　　■ Third sixth　　□ Below average

England-only maps

Failing to obtain five or more GCSEs
Failure to obtain five or more GCSEs is most common in urban areas.

The map shows how the number of students (defined as pupils aged 15 at 31 August in the calendar year prior to sitting the exams) failing to obtain five or more GCSEs varies by upper tier local authority. The data includes both those who do not enter for exams and those who do enter but obtain less than five.

The data source is DfES performance tables and the data is for 2003/04. The data covers all maintained schools.

Underage pregnancies
Underage pregnancies are most common in urban areas and, with some exceptions, generally follow similar patterns to failure to obtain five or more GCSEs.

The map shows how the number of conceptions per year to girls conceiving under the age of 16 varies by upper tier local authority. Note that small sample sizes mean that each authority's figures will be subject to some uncertainty and, to improve statistical reliability, the data is averaged over the years 1998 to 2002.

The data source is DH3 mortality statistics from ONS. The numerator is the average number of conceptions in a year and the denominator is the total number of girls aged 13 to 15.

Older people not being helped to live at home
The local authorities who help the fewest of their older citizens to live at home are outside of the cities, across southern England, East Anglia and Yorkshire.

The map shows how the proportion of people being helped to live at home varies by local authority district. The data is expressed per 1,000 population aged 75 and over on the grounds that the majority of people being helped to live at home are aged 75 or over. Note that 'being helped to live at home' is a wider measure than the 'receiving home help/care' as it includes meals-on-wheels, day care etc.

The data source is the Audit Commission Best Value Performance Indicators (England). The data is for 2003/04.

Homelessness
Though worst in London and the North East, both rural and urban areas anywhere in the country can have serious problems of homelessness.

The map shows how the proportion of households who were accepted as statutory homeless by their local authority varies by local authority district. It includes both those 'in priority need' and those 'not in priority need' but excludes those deemed to be intentionally homeless (a relatively small number).

The data source is ODPM published quarterly statistics on homelessness. The numerator is the total number of households accepted as statutory homeless in 2004 and the denominator is the total number of households as estimated by ODPM.